**BLACK BELT**
P R E S E N T S

# THE BEST OF
# DAVE LOWRY

## KARATE WAY COLUMNS
## 1995 to 2005

**BLACK BELT®**
**PRESENTS**

# THE BEST OF DAVE LOWRY

**KARATE WAY COLUMNS • 1995 to 2005**

Compiled by Jon Thibault

Edited by Raymond Horwitz,
Jeannine Santiago and Jon Thibault

Graphic Design by John Bodine

Illustrations by Jaimie Filer

©2005 Black Belt Communications LLC
All Rights Reserved
Printed in the United States of America
Library of Congress Control Number: 2005926571
ISBN 0-89750-148-9

*First Printing 2005*

## WARNING

This book is presented only as a means of preserving a unique aspect of the heritage of the martial arts. Neither Ohara Publications nor the author make any representation, warranty or guarantee that the techniques described or illustrated in this book will be safe or effective in any self-defense situation or otherwise. You may be injured if you apply or train in the techniques illustrated in this book and neither Ohara Publications nor the author is responsible for any such injury that may result. It is essential that you consult a physician regarding whether or not to attempt any technique described in this book. Specific self-defense responses illustrated in this book may not be justified in any particular situation in view of all of the circumstances or under applicable federal, state or local law. Neither Ohara Publications nor the author make any representation or warranty regarding the legality or appropriateness of any technique mentioned in this book.

**BLACK BELT BOOKS**
A Division of **OHARA PUBLICATIONS, INC.**
*World Leader in Martial Arts Publications*

## ABOUT THE AUTHOR

Since 1968, Dave Lowry has been an avid student and practitioner of several Japanese martial arts. He has trained in *karate-do*, judo and *aikido*, and he is an exponent of the *shindo muso-ryu* and the *yagyu shinkage-ryu*, two classical schools of combat that date back to Japan's feudal era.

Lowry is a longtime contributor to *Black Belt* and has written a monthly column since 1986. His articles have appeared in several publications in the United States, Japan and Great Britain, including *Cosmopolitan*, *Playboy*, *Bottom Line* and *Winds*, the in-flight magazine of Japan Airlines. Lowry is also the restaurant critic for *St. Louis Magazine*.

He is the author of nine books, and his latest, *The Connoisseur's Guide to Sushi*, will be published later this year. Lowry lives and trains near St. Louis.

# TABLE OF CONTENTS

# FOREWORD

When I began my martial arts training in the late 1960s, *Black Belt* was one of the few English-language publications devoted to the subject. I remember the first issue I saw—in fact, I still have it, worn and faded. Thumbing through the now-yellowed pages makes me realize what a different world we now live in. The best *keikogi* money could buy back then was advertised in the magazine for less than $20. The faces in the pictures are mostly Asian. Though there were Caucasians practicing judo, *karate-do*, *kendo* and *aikido* in those days, we were definitely a minority in most locales.

When I began writing for *Black Belt* and its sister publication *Karate Illustrated* in the late 1970s, I was still largely a product of that earlier generation. Paying $100 or more for training clothes seemed bizarre, and I would never have dreamed that someday there would be more people practicing martial arts in the United States than in Japan.

Perhaps I reached geezerhood earlier than most, because I started writing for *Black Belt* from the perspective of that earlier era. I was surprised when the magazine first accepted my work—it seemed very much out of sync with the flashy razzmatazz of musical *kata* and rainbow-hued keikogi, of full-contact championships and glitzy martial arts movies. I was writing about ancient traditions and archaic notions, yet they continued to print my work.

Most of the time, I suspect the subjects I tackle are utterly foreign to the editors, and they no doubt find certain topics boring. I bet they even disagree with some of what I've written. I can't imagine that very many of today's readers buy the magazine owing to my columns, so it's not as if I'm making the publisher wealthy. Nevertheless, for more than two decades, *Black Belt* has given me a vehicle to write about the old ways, the old arts, the old traditions, and now they have generously taken on the task of selecting some of those columns for this book. You have my gratitude for reading it, and the editors and staff at *Black Belt* have my gratitude for allowing me to express my ideas for all these years.

—*Dave Lowry*
*April 2005*

# TAKE A DEEP BREATH

*February 1995*

L ay down flat on your back. Put one hand on your abdomen. Now breathe in and out.

What happened? If your hand rose and fell with your respiration, you are breathing correctly.

It may seem odd to think of breathing incorrectly. After all, we have been breathing all our lives without instruction. But the truth is that very few of us breathe in a way that promotes health and relaxation. Most of us, because of a combination of high-stress lifestyles, poor posture and sitting long hours in chairs, tend to breathe shallowly through our chests.

The martial disciplines of Japan feature a wide range of instruction on proper breathing. It's usually referred to as *kokyu* or *ibuki*. Some, like the Okinawan schools of karate, may advocate forced, muscular respiration patterns. Mainland Japanese martial systems tend to be more natural in their breathing methods. In some classical fighting styles, special instructions are given to advanced students to facilitate respiration during battle. The fundamental aspect of all these methods involves breathing from the diaphragm, the band of muscle below your lungs. That is why the martial artist is often said to "breathe from his belly."

To practice this technique, sit up straight on the floor, legs crossed or bent beneath you in the *seiza* position. Keep your posture straight but not rigid. Breathe in slowly—not loudly but naturally. There should be no sound. Don't force the inhalation down. Let it sink, as if your belly is spreading out to make space for it. When you exhale, gently squeeze the air out, tightening your abdominal muscles. Once again, don't be hard or forceful. This should be abdominal, diaphragmatic breathing.

Abdominal breathing is the basis for all forms of respiration in the Japanese martial arts. To be philosophical about it, we might say it is breathing from the *hara*, the spot below the navel, which in traditional Japanese thought is regarded as the body's spiritual center and physical core.

Interestingly, abdominal breathing occurs in every type of Japanese art. *Noh* and *kabuki* actors practice it to improve their speaking and singing. An *itamae* (sushi chef) once showed me how to cut thick fish fillets with a single stroke of a knife. It is an art, believe me. "Of course, unless you are breathing from your hara, it's impossible to do," he said.

To perform or practice karate or any of the other Japanese martial arts correctly, proper breathing is essential. Without a strong emphasis on developing abdominal respiration, the chances of perfecting your martial art are, like the itamae said, impossible.

# A REAL MASTER

*March 1995*

Sometimes, I'm sorry to say, today's great karate masters are seen by many American *karateka* as mere stationary figures in instruction books. Yet these masters are very much alive and possess unique personalities.

Keigo Abe, one of the senior instructors of the Japan Karate Association (JKA), is such a man. Although he long ago retired from tournament competition, he is one of the most respected karate masters on earth. He is particularly renowned for his skill at fighting at close range—a distance that gives many karate stylists trouble. Abe has an uncanny ability to entice a strong attack from his opponents, then pivot away from it while lashing out a backfist that his oncoming adversary literally runs into.

Like many karate practitioners who matured right after World War II, Abe's karate is infused with a deep sense of *yamato damashi*—the "Japanese spirit"—which can be distinguished by a profound patriotism, as well as an intensity in martial arts training and competition that borders on the sadistic. Abe recalls his early karate training as being "very hard," with entire sessions of continuous punching while in the straddle-legged *kiba dachi* stance.

"Every day we did five-step sparring that was almost like free fighting. It was just like a fight," says Abe, who claims this kind of vigorous train-

---

**[Keigo] Abe has an uncanny ability to entice a strong attack from his opponents, then pivot away from it while lashing out a backfist that his oncoming adversary literally runs into.**

---

ing helped him in tournament competition. During the 1960s and '70s, he was a member of the powerful JKA national team. No one who saw these legendary martial artists in action can ever feel comfortable referring to traditional karate tournaments as "noncontact" events.

Abe also inherited an interest in swords and swordsmanship from his samurai ancestors, whose home was once invaded by two thieves. "My family killed them," he says. "The two graves are still standing near my house."

Abe not only collects *katana* (Japanese swords) and practices *muso shinden-ryu* sword-drawing techniques, he was one of the sword-wielding warriors in the James Bond movie *You Only Live Twice*.

A graduate of Nihon University in Japan and an instructor with the

JKA, Abe says of his approach to karate, "I believe karate must be like a real fight—to feel, even when practicing alone, that you are facing an opponent. Some teachers say that, when you block, you don't have to feel pain yourself. But for me, I want to feel the pain."

Abe knows what he is talking about. Back in his university days, he had several encounters with tough guys. He kicked one attacker squarely in the nose (so much for the arguments about the effectiveness of high kicks in self-defense). Abe was wearing wooden *geta* sandals at the time, and the kick did so much damage to his attacker's nose that extensive reconstructive surgery was needed to restore it.

And what does this dangerous karate master do to relax?

"I perform tea ceremonies," he says.

# TIMING IN COMBAT

*May 1995*

The study of karate includes two broad means of improving one's timing for combat. They are *sen no sen*, meaning "early advantage," and *go no sen*, meaning "delayed advantage." These sen, or "intervals," can be thought of as the space—mental and physical—between the opportunity for an attack and the implementation of that attack.

Sen no sen involves taking the initiative in a fight—delivering a strike before your opponent can prepare an assault. In a real confrontation, this can mean attacking the opponent the moment he says, "You wanna start somethin'?" While one must be aware of the legal and philosophical ramifications of this kind of response on the streets, it can be practiced safely and effectively in the *dojo*.

Assuming that you're prepared for an attack in a training environment, how does your partner set you up for sen no sen? Basically, there are two ways: *tai no sen* and *yu no sen*, both of which can be considered subsets of sen no sen. Tai no sen calls for your adversary to charge directly, but not mindlessly, toward you. Tai no sen is not like a suicide charge; instead, the opponent must control his actions from the beginning, while your movements will be completely defensive as you play catch-up.

Tai no sen creates an environment in which, owing to your defense-oriented stand, you are vulnerable to a direct attack. From the moment

---

*Tai no sen* **is not like a suicide charge; instead, the opponent must control his actions from the beginning, while your movements will be completely defensive as you play catch-up.**

---

the encounter begins, your opponent is consciously trying to dominate you. His attacks come on a more or less linear path. Think of him as having a long, thick pole that he is pushing against your abdomen and using to drive you backward. If his push is strong and steady enough, you will be unable to find the balance or reflexes to resist or to mount a counterattack.

Yu no sen, the other aspect of sen no sen, also involves a kind of domination in strategy. The attacks in yu no sen, however, are indirect. Your training partner should begin with a feint, such as a punch to your face, which causes you to lean backward. Your legs now exposed, your partner follows with a foot sweep, then a front kick and the technique he plans to score with—another punch to your face. This strategy involves indirect attacks, or yu no sen.

It may be said that tai no sen requires a decisive use of speed, while yu no sen demands a perfection in distancing. In truth, however, either of these manifestations of sen no sen are impossible without a foundation in all the karate basics: distancing, speed and the application of explosive power.

Next month, we will take up the subject of go no sen, the skill known as "delayed advantage."

# WAITING FOR THE KILL

*June 1995*

The Japanese term *sen* refers to the interval between the opportunity for and implementation of the attack. There are basically two types of sen—*sen no sen* (early advantage) and *go no sen* (delayed advantage). Last issue (May 1995), you were introduced to the concept of sen no sen, and this month you will learn about its complement, go no sen, the strategy of waiting to attack.

You engage in go no sen (also called *ato no sen*; go and *ato* both mean "after" or "later") when your opponent has attacked and you are counterattacking. Go no sen is vulnerable to all sorts of misinterpretations. If sen no sen is misinterpreted as "aggressive" initiative, then logically, go no sen is perceived as more "passive." This has led many karate stylists to assume that, when implementing go no sen, they must wait and deal with an incoming attack and try to respond to the situation. Such an attitude is bound to lead to failure. In a real-life situation, it is a potentially lethal approach.

To adopt the attitude of go no sen in an encounter is to manipulate the action without the opponent knowing that he is being controlled. True, your opponent "initiates" the attack, but if you're employing go no sen correctly, it will be the kind of strike you want him to make. You will therefore be able to anticipate his attack and use it to prepare your counter.

---

**Like the chess expert, the karate practitioner initiating *go no sen* should always think a few moves ahead.**

---

The expert in go no sen will purposely deceive his opponent. He will provide an opening in his stance, his movements or his distancing. He will move backward, hold his guard high and perhaps entice his opponent to kick him. Your adversary will discover that you have put too much space between the two of you to make a hand strike effective. And your high guard will tempt him into aiming a kick at your midsection. However, by the time he has begun to take the bait, you have moved again, closing in, dropping your hands to grab the kick, and then counterattacking with your own technique.

Go no sen is the strategy of a chess master. Like the chess expert, the karate practitioner initiating go no sen should always think a few moves ahead. He offers a pawn to his opponent but keeps a knight in reserve,

THE BEST OF DAVE LOWRY

ready to strike at his adversary the moment he moves in.

This strategy might sound simple, but you will discover that, even if you give your opponent an opening, you shouldn't assume he will always respond in a specific manner. Many times, the opponent isn't so obliging. He has his own ideas and agenda. Instead of delivering the kick you had hoped for, he may change tactics, drop his guard and try to lure you into an attack.

The solution to this and other problems encountered in go no sen come only after years of study and practice. The karate student must work not only to control his opponent's physical moves but also his mind and spirit. The karate practitioner must master the art of waiting, but not waiting in a passive sense. Go no sen is "active" waiting. Waiting for the kill.

# DUTIES OF THE SENIOR KARATE STUDENT
*August 1995*

What responsibilities do the senior students have at a karate school?

It is an important question. Unfortunately, too many karate schools encourage a "me first" attitude, and the senior students are worried only about their own personal development. Juniors are seen as either a burden or as moving punching bags. I have heard of schools where seniors prepare for competition by lining up a string of their juniors and using them as sparring partners.

These attitudes are despicable. The true martial artist treats juniors like younger siblings. A good karate practitioner knows that the strength of the school, and the strength of his art, rests on the next generation, and he therefore cares for it with diligence.

Spending time with juniors is only part of the responsibility of being a senior karate student. Another duty is the constant evaluation of the juniors' skill and the ability to adjust to that level during practice. Consider, for example, a junior who is working on sidestepping a front kick, while his

---

**A good karate practitioner knows that the strength of the school, and the strength of his art, rests on the next generation, and he therefore cares for it with diligence.**

---

senior partner is repeatedly performing the kick for him to dodge. A self-centered senior will use this session as an opportunity to practice his technique, uncorking one powerful kick after another. A more mature senior, however, will adjust his kicks. He will unleash some completely beyond the junior's capability to defend, and then he will ease up and deliver kicks with an almost lazy energy, allowing the junior to avoid them. This helps the junior get a feel for the technique and makes him feel competent.

The senior might then step it up a level, increase his kicking speed and begin to press the junior, challenging him to improve his defenses. The senior will kick faster and harder until he reaches the junior's limit, then he'll back off again, but not quite as much as before.

At the same time, the senior is not neglecting his own training. When he is executing kicks at the slower speeds, he is evaluating his own kicking form. Is his knee cocked correctly? Is his hip thrusting forward? The senior is honing his own techniques while seeing to the instructional needs of those below him.

The senior must also remember that, just as he evaluates the juniors in class, they are watching him. They will notice whether a male senior rushes to help an attractive female junior while ignoring male beginners. They will be observant of the senior's attendance habits and will notice whether he is frequently absent. They will notice whether the senior shows respect for his instructor and his *dojo*. And they will notice whether the senior lives the precepts of his art, and whether its values are translated into his actions, both in and out of the training hall.

It is not easy to be a senior karate student. It is very similar to the painful, difficult process of growing up and realizing there is a younger generation behind you that trusts you for its care. It is up to the seniors not to disappoint these individuals.

# WARNING:
# MARTIAL ARTS TRAINING CAN BE HABIT-FORMING

*February 1996*

The fortunate person learns that true happiness in life can only be achieved through constant dedication to disciplined habit in daily living. Only when a person is able to willingly undertake a pattern of living in which he deprives himself of all excesses can he find a content and balanced life, and his function on Earth be said to be fulfilled.

*—Koun Suhara*

Koun Suhara is a senior priest at the Engakuji, the Zen Buddhist temple where *shotokan* karate founder Gichin Funakoshi is interred. In addition to his duties as a priest, Suhara is an enthusiastic practitioner of *kyudo* (archery) and *iaido* (sword drawing). The preceding quote eloquently describes the concept of what the Japanese call *tsune*—training as a "daily habit."

Tsune is a word usually applied to such matters as brushing one's teeth or attending to other routine daily activities. In terms of *budo*, it refers to the level of experience and involvement in which the training process becomes so integrated into one's lifestyle that it becomes a daily routine. When the *budoka* reaches a point at which he practices his art as a tsune, it is almost certain that he will continue his training for the rest of his life.

Before the tsune stage, the budoka often struggles with his training. Not only is he dealing with the acquisition of technical skills, he must fight to make the practice schedule fit into the fabric of his life. This is not as easy as it sounds. There is an endless parade of excuses available for not going to the martial arts studio: illness, work, fatigue, family obligations, etc. Or perhaps the practitioner is simply lazy and unmotivated. Such excuses emerge like bubbles in a pot of boiling water when it comes time to go to the *dojo*. Other times, the would-be budoka is quite serious about his training, yet something always comes up that gets in the way of his attendance at martial arts class. In a way, this period of training is something of a test for the martial artist, and many will fail. Their lives are never able to accommodate regular training.

For those who persevere, however, there is the discovery of tsune. It happens gradually. Without realizing it, the martial arts suddenly become part of the practitioner's daily routine. He no longer consciously thinks about it—at least no more than he would think about making his bed or taking out the trash. In fact, if he misses a training session, it's as if something is wrong. It's like forgetting to wash his clothes or turn on the porch light in the evening. The practitioner has, at this point, woven the martial arts into his life, and it will remain part of his existence until the day he dies.

# LEARN BY NOT DOING

*April 1996*

A practice method I've encountered more than once in Japanese karate schools, but rarely see in the United States, involves an unusual way of perfecting a technique—by not doing it.

Well, that's not exactly accurate, but it's close. What this practice method attempts to do is isolate the many components in a technique. A good way to explain it is by using as an example a front kick performed from the *zenkutsu dachi* front stance with the back leg. After you've warmed up, perform the kick 30 to 40 times, enough to get the muscles used to the movement. Then execute the kick again, except at the very last instant, instead of curling your toes back to push the ball of the foot forward, simply let the foot go slack. In other words, complete all the actions of the kick except for the last one. Repeat the kick this way 30 to 40 times.

Next, perform the same kick, but leave off both the last movement and the penultimate movement—the extension of the lower half of the leg. Now you're concentrating just on driving the knee up toward the target. Do you see where this is heading? If you liken the technique to a length

> If you liken the technique to a length of chain, you are gradually removing links, breaking it down so it can be studied piece by piece.

of chain, you are gradually removing links, breaking it down so it can be studied piece by piece.

The next link to go is the kicking leg itself. Drive your hip from the 45-degree angle of the front stance to a fully front-facing direction. But keep your kicking foot on the floor. Study the movement of the hips and torso at this point. Are they snapping forward at the same time, as they should?

Next, try squeezing together the thigh muscles involved in the kick. At this stage, the only movement you'll be making is a strong twitching as the thigh muscles tense. You should be concentrating on exploring the relationship of the front, non-kicking leg to the back leg that actually performs the kick. And remember, you should perform an equal number of repetitions of each of these gradually abbreviated techniques.

You can continue to isolate the movements of the front kick until you are down to just tensing the toes of the supporting foot. Concentrate entirely on them. Where is the weight distribution along the length of your foot? What is the connection between the vertical movement of the toes squeezing in and down the lateral rotation of the heel?

At the Japan Karate Association headquarters in Tokyo, this kind of training is common, and when it is applied to several basic techniques, an entire class session may be spent without executing a single technique all the way through. Instead, the focus is placed on mastering individual elements, broken down in such a scientific manner, that make up the whole technique.

Try this kind of training from time to time. It's a sure way to learn the fine points that will make your technique stronger. It's also a way to isolate or accentuate any problems you might be having.

# KARATE'S THREE ELEMENTS OF SUCCESS

*May 1996*

If you've ever had the privilege of watching some of the great Japanese karate experts who developed their skills shortly after World War II, you probably witnessed some spectacular skills. These guys are awesome. Their incredible abilities are no doubt attributable to incessant hard work, superior instruction and so forth, but the majority of these Japanese *karateka* share another commonality. Because it is so popular in Japan, most Japanese karate masters have had training in *kendo*.

Kendo, the "way of the sword," offers a different perspective on karate practice, and it is regrettable that more students don't have the time or opportunity to pursue it.

Karate practitioners can learn a great deal about striking by engaging in kendo training. In a kendo *shiai* (tournament), the referee looks for three essentials in a strike that will distinguish it from the flurry of ineffective blows often seen in such contests. When he spots all three elements in a strike, he knows it represents an attack worthy of a winning point. These elements are described as *ki-ken-tai*.

*Ki*, in this sense, refers to the spirit or willful intention behind the strike. It does not come by accident or luck (although at very advanced levels,

---

**In a *kendo shiai* (tournament), the referee looks for three essentials in a strike that will distinguish it from the flurry of ineffective blows often seen in such contests.**

---

kendo practitioners will seem to score exactly that way, as if by effortless serendipity, and a referee, unless he's very good, can actually miss seeing the point). To strike with ki is to make a conscious decision to attack, to commit fully to the strike. The referee watches for a sense of deliberate determination by the competitor—not overt aggression or a fanatic *kamikaze* charge, but a calm, reasoned commitment to the score. That is ki.

*Ken* is the element of the sword itself. Is it being held and wielded correctly? Is there a solid connection made with the cutting portion of the *shinai*—the bamboo sword used in kendo? If you have ever fooled around with a shinai, you know it is an easy weapon with which to whack away. But the results are often more slaps than effective attacks. It is actually quite difficult to connect with sufficient technique, power and speed to warrant

THE BEST OF DAVE LOWRY

a point in a kendo match. Ken is the proper alchemy of all these factors.

*Tai* is the Japanese term for the body. Within ki-ken-tai, it is a component that encompasses many things, including posture, body connection and coordination. In the early days of kendo, a point would never have been called if the aggressor's heel was off the ground at the moment of impact—and for an entirely logical reason. Power is transmitted through the body via a solid connection with the ground, at least according to the kinesiology of the Japanese *budo*. If the practitioner's heel is raised, there is a break in that connection and a consequent disruption in power delivery. Tightening the shoulders will also disrupt the flow of power, as will sticking out the rear end. These all represent mistakes in tai, and if the referee notices them—and rest assured he will—he will recognize that, even if the blow lands, it will not warrant a point.

You've probably noticed by now how the principles of ki-ken-tai also apply to karate. The applications of karate and kendo are very similar. In both arts, ki-ken-tai must be present (and in the order they're listed) for an attack to be effective. Volition—the conscious will to strike—must come first (ki), followed by proper use of the weapon or fist (ken). The body and posture must back up all of the action (tai). It does not matter whether the art is kendo or karate. Ki-ken-tai, the essentials for success, are the same.

# SPIRIT: HOW IMPORTANT IS IT?

*July 1996*

Much has been said in martial arts circles about the importance of "spirit," perhaps because many Westerners perceive the traditional Japanese/Okinawan martial arts as a means for the weak to overcome the strong. Perhaps it is because these arts are often presented in exhibitions that feature individuals doing the seemingly impossible—breaking great stacks of boards, successfully warding off multiple attackers, and leaping head-high into the air to deliver spectacular kicks. Many of the feats in karate seem to defy the laws of physics. It has become ingrained in many people—karate practitioners and the general public alike—that karate is some kind of mystical art.

Japanese karate teachers, at a loss to explain in English how much of karate actually works, have further clouded the issue. You have to have strong spirit, they tell their students. The implications behind this statement are varied and can be extremely misleading.

By "spirit," I think most of these teachers are actually referring to "attitude." You must have the correct attitude to do anything properly. And in the *budo*, proper attitude is particularly essential for several reasons. First, it is impossible to accomplish much in any martial discipline in a short period of time. After six months of karate training, a beginner may be able to make a fist correctly—and that's about it. He may have begun to polish some elementary stances and perhaps even a basic *kata*. But at this stage, he is really just imitating what he sees his teacher or seniors doing. He has no real ability yet, and if he's smart, he'll realize this and be frustrated by it. If he has the wrong attitude, this is the point at which he'll lose interest. If his attitude is correct and he realizes the long road before him, he will persevere and move forward.

Second, spirit (or proper attitude) is vital to learning the budo, which is a foreign enterprise to most new students, who therefore need to have absolute faith in their teachers. So in this sense, spirit is a form of trust and an acceptance of the rules and training laid down by the instructor. It is a willingness to do things his way with the sincere belief that you will eventually understand what's going on.

However, some teachers can place so much emphasis on developing the correct spirit that they present a lopsided view of the budo. The truth is that all the spirit in the world cannot take you to the summits of the martial arts unless you also have correct instruction. You may train eight hours a day and execute 10,000 front kicks and 20,000 punches, but if you are not shown how to perform those kicks and punches properly, you are largely wasting your time. Although spirit is important, you must have a technical foundation, as well, or you're merely spinning your wheels.

As I mentioned, Westerners have come to believe that the martial arts can provide some kind of almost magical power, and we often neglect the details—the technical aspects that make the final product look and work as good as it does. One of the details in mastering karate or other budo is securing expert instruction. Unfortunately, a great many "teachers" are nothing of the sort. Some are outright impostors, while others have been taught incorrectly themselves, yet have been granted permission by their own ineffective teachers to instruct students. Both types of instructors, either deliberately or unconsciously, develop a wide repertoire of psychological stratagems to keep students.

One of their tactics is to make a big deal about the importance of spirit in training: "*Sensei*, I just can't make this kick work; it doesn't have any power. What am I doing wrong?"

"Not enough spirit! Practice harder!"

If the ersatz teacher has sufficient charisma and acting ability, he can dress up this message with dramatics that inspire the student to double his enthusiasm and output. But it still won't do the student any good because his teacher is incapable of supplying the right kind of instruction. The instructor cannot improve the student's kick because he just plain doesn't know how to do it himself, or he doesn't know how to communicate the information.

The real crime here is that, not only does the student not learn or improve, he also thinks his shortcomings are his fault. The karate teacher is deliberately placing the burden of guilt on the student instead of putting it where it belongs—on himself. Anyone so venal as to pass himself off as a legitimate martial arts instructor is unlikely to lose any sleep over this, but it illustrates just how damaging bogus instruction can be. The student probably came to the *dojo* in the first place because he had a poor self-image, was afraid of being attacked, or was unable to cope with stressful situations. And a bad teacher can actually reinforce these feelings.

It doesn't matter how many times or how energetically you hit the nail; if you're using the wrong end of the hammer, you're not going to get the job done. Karate training is the same way. Foster a strong spirit in all aspects of your life, including your attitude about karate, and then make sure you have a teacher who is worthy of directing it.

# MAY THE FORCE—AND POWER—BE WITH YOU

*August 1996*

If you're going to get anywhere in the martial arts, you must give some very serious thought to the difference between force and power. If you fail to understand the distinction between these two entities, you will reach a certain skill level, become frustrated and progress no further. You might start to feel that your chosen art is just too difficult or complex to be mastered by the likes of you, or maybe you will decide that your system is just a sham.

Force is energy exerted against an opponent (or, at much higher levels of training, against oneself) without an awareness of, or connection to, that opponent. Here's an example: Take a long pole, extend it horizontally in front of you, and start twirling around. As you and the pole spin like a helicopter blade, what would happen if I walked into the stick's path? Your force would do some damage. But what if, while spinning, your stick struck a tree? The energy you were exerting would come barreling right back down the stick and into you, and you would absorb the damaging shock. You will have learned a lesson in the limitations of force.

Now, let's say you swung the stick like a baseball bat against me. You could probably do even more damage this way because your aim and the path of striking would be deliberate rather than random. Further, let's say I was so strong that I could, like that tree, absorb your strike without moving. You could actually use the energy that would be coming back at you for a follow-up strike. By redirecting the energy, you could drive the other end of the pole at me from a different angle. That is power.

Power, in terms of the martial arts, is the ability to exert energy with some sense of how it will be received, coupled with the flexibility to redirect that energy if it is stopped or redirected by the opponent. Some martial arts, such as *aikido*, accentuate this aspect of training. That's why, when you begin aikido practice, you will spend many months learning the principles of motion and control against an opponent who is using various attacks against you. Wrist grabs and other holds provide a connection with your opponent in practice. You can actually feel his strength and the direction of his energy. Only much later does the aikido practitioner begin to deal with strikes and other attacks that come from a greater distance.

The karate practitioner has a much more difficult path in learning to generate power. Unfortunately, poor and unqualified instruction in the art is still the rule in the Western world. Many karate students in North

America are led to believe that force is the same as power (perhaps it's more accurate to say that no one ever explains the difference to them). Their force usually works until, inevitably, they run into someone with greater force, or worse, they run into someone who understands power.

Karate does possess several exercises to promote the development of power. You can use the most basic *kata* to this end. *Heian shodan's* third movement consists of a downward block, followed by a rising hammerfist strike. After executing the block, have a partner grab your wrist. Perform the rising strike as an escape technique. Then repeat the steps, with your partner performing the grab from a different angle or with a reversed grip. Closely observe how your body moves in relation to your arm. Does the hip retract before the arms swing back, or after?

You will find similar opportunities for these kinds of attacks and responses elsewhere in heian shodan and in other kata. Each directional change offers an opportunity to pull away from a grab and study the mechanics of exerting power as opposed to merely learning the limitations of force.

# THE BLACK-BELT INITIATION

*November 1996*

The period immediately following a karate practitioner's promotion into the ranks of the *yudansha*, or "black-belt holders," is a critical one. He may believe he has reached a conclusion of sorts, or has "graduated" from the lower ranks. He may fall victim to cockiness and adopt an arrogant air of superiority. He may strut and behave in the most irritating and condescending way to his own juniors. In fact, a newly promoted black belt can be a real pain in the behind.

A great majority of new black belts may be deeply troubled by their promotions. The prospective black belt often regards the *kuro no obi* wrapped around the waist of his seniors as a kind of talisman—a rank he can only dream of attaining. Then, before he knows it, he is testing for his own black belt. He passes, and he lines up for his first class with his new black belt knotted around him. This can be quite disconcerting for him. After all, he knows he hasn't learned the secrets to combative invincibility. He isn't the martial arts wonder he always believed black belts to be. He feels like a bit of a fraud, and he wonders whether the promotion was a mistake.

The new black belt is at an important stage in his training. A wise teacher will recognize this and deal with it. One of the best ways of tackling this situation is to institute in the *dojo* a kind of initiation that comes after the testing session. There is a saying in Japanese that after *shinsa* (testing) should come *shinsan* (privation or suffering). Shinsan should not be confused with hazing or other forms of abuse. An initiation should not be punishment. The idea is to demonstrate to the new black belts that they have earned their promotions and they are different, in many important ways, from the people they were when they first walked into the dojo. The purpose of an initiation is to show them that they are worthy of the rank in a clear and physical way.

The teacher should try to set aside a weekend for such an event. If that's not possible, the initiation should last at least the better part of a day. The shinsan should be an intense practice session (but not a survival course) covering all the basic areas of karate training, from *kihon* (basic techniques) to *kata* to *kumite*.

A typical initiation might go something like this:

• **7:30 a.m. to 9:30 a.m.:** Kihon practice. This serves as a warm-up session. Students begin slowly, and they gradually increase their speed and power. The workout includes downward blocks followed by step-in

punches, rising blocks followed by step-in punches, front kicks with
reverse punches, knifehand blocks in a back stance followed by front
kicks off the forward leg, midlevel blocks in a front stance followed by

reverse backfists, and step-in front kicks followed by reverse punches. The instructor then should have students repeat the sequences, using their opposite hands and feet. The complexity of the combinations should gradually increase, and the teacher should be sure to include techniques that require backward motion, as well.

• **9:30 a.m. to 11:30 a.m.:** Kata. Instructors begin with the first kata they teach—usually *heian* or *pinan shodan*—and work forward. Students should begin slowly, using little power or focus in the techniques, and then step it up as they repeat the moves. This is not a time for instruction or correction.

• **11:30 a.m. to 1:00 p.m.:** Lunch.

• **1:00 p.m. to 1:30 p.m.:** Stretching and warm-up.

• **1:30 p.m. to 2:30 p.m.:** *Yakusoku* kumite, which consists of one-, two- and three-step techniques. The instructors can also include more complex exchanges, such as five-step kumite, if they are a normal part of the training regimen.

• **2:30 p.m. to 4:30 p.m.:** *Jiyu* kumite—a free exchange of techniques. The new black belts face an opponent who is not part of the initiation. There should be more opponents than new black belts so that the opponents can be periodically rotated and remain fresh during kumite practice, while the new black belts must continue fighting for the entire session. Students must be sure to exercise control over their techniques during this part of the initiation. The new black belts will be tired and on edge by this time. They may be able to perform a halfhearted kata and still look ok—but against a live opponent, they must give a sincere effort. In their eagerness to do so, they will be tempted to "go wild." Instructors should explain to the new black belts that, in real life, confrontations and emergencies don't happen when you're calm and well-rested. Control is easy in peaceful interludes, but karate practitioners must demonstrate the same control in the midst of considerable agitation.

• **4:30 p.m. to 5:00 p.m.:** Stretching. Instructors should finish the initiation with a series of slow, sustained stretching drills. Then, using the palms of their hands, students should massage their muscles, concentrating on the inner thighs and inner arms, both above and below the elbows.

No matter how an initiation class is conducted, the goal remains the same. The *karateka* must see for themselves that they have earned the rank they wear, and this is perhaps the most valuable thing a new black belt can learn.

# THE RHYTHM OF KATA

*December 1996*

When polishing a *kata*, the karate practitioner must pay particular attention to the matter of rhythm. I am speaking here, of course, about those practitioners who have already learned the sequence of the kata and understand how the various techniques are put together. When you have progressed to this point in your training, you are ready to move on to some of the more advanced elements of kata, one of which is rhythm.

Karate, as you may know, is one of the few Japanese combat arts that employ solo training for kata. The *ko-ryu*, or martial arts of the Japanese feudal period, all utilize two-man kata practice, as do modern judo and *kendo*. In two-man situations, rhythm develops naturally. The more senior exponent usually plays the "attacker" and sets the rhythm of the kata, making it easier for the junior student to assimilate this concept.

The karate practitioner, however, must learn rhythm in kata by observation and constant thinking because he has no partner to work with. He observes his instructor and senior students and then emulates them. He must also thoroughly understand the nature of the kata movements, their applications, where the targets are and what he's defending against. All of these considerations will influence the kata's rhythm.

A true understanding of a *kata's* rhythm is centered around understanding why techniques are grouped as they are.

At levels below black belt, the karate practitioner will not have a strong understanding of rhythm and generally will perform kata in a metronomic fashion: one-two-three. Even movements obviously designed to be executed slowly, like the opening techniques of the *heian yondan* kata, will be performed by the lower-ranked student with little regard for the rhythm of combat. But as the karate practitioner ascends to more advanced levels, he will begin to see that moves he thought were performed as "one-two-three" are actually executed as "one ... two-three" or "one-two ... three." He will eventually realize that the opponents he is confronting within the framework of the kata are being met at slightly different intervals.

If this level of kata practice is attempted too soon or without supervision, the practitioner will simply be "playing pretend" by imagining opponents coming at different speeds and making up his timing in response. However, a true understanding of a kata's rhythm is centered around understanding why techniques are grouped as they are.

For example, the first kata that karate students usually learn is heian *shodan*. It begins with a downward block, followed by a step-in punch. The beginner will perform these maneuvers as two separate movements. The real rhythm of these two techniques, however, finds the opening block flowing into the following strike. This maneuver is, of course, easier to explain in words than it is to perform correctly. If the practitioner attempts to blend the two techniques too soon in his training, he will simply "slur" the movements together with no focus.

If, however, you are introduced to this concept correctly, you will see in the rhythm of these two simple techniques a new world open up in your practice. For instance, this is the exact rhythm used for nerve strikes—stimulating the region with one move (the block) and then enervation with the strike. It is the same rhythm necessary to set up a foot sweep/strike combination. It is no exaggeration to say that an entire seminar could be built around this simple move from the most elementary of karate kata. It's all a matter of rhythm.

# A WARRIOR'S LESSON
January 1997

"The first quality of a soldier is consistency in the endurance of fatigue and hardship."

—Napoleon Bonaparte

There was an incident at the Atlanta Olympic Games that probably went unnoticed by most individuals. It involved judo player David Khakhaleichvili of the Republic of Georgia, who was scheduled to defend the heavyweight title he won at the 1992 games in Barcelona, Spain. The incident in question did not occur on the mat, nor did it involve an error in technique or strategy. In fact, Khakhaleichvili didn't even compete; he missed the train to the stadium.

Khakhaleichvili is one of the dominant players in international judo competition, and he was expected to dominate and remain a champion. But when he reported to the weigh-in room the morning of his first match, he discovered the weigh-ins were being held at another site, clear across the city.

Khakhaleichvili got on a train. He wasn't able to understand much English, and he missed the sign announcing his stop. He eventually discovered the mistake, turned around, and got off at the right place. But on

---

**If you can't get to the battlefield, if you're too sick or sore or hungry to fight once you get there, if you can't communicate effectively with your teammates, it probably won't matter how skilled you are or how long you've trained.**

---

trying to enter the building where the weigh-ins were being conducted, he found he had forgotten his Olympic credentials and was denied access. He was forced to return to his room and retrieve his ID, but by the time he returned, he had missed the weigh-in and forfeited his match to his Romanian opponent.

"I don't know if I want to live anymore," Khakhaleichvili later told reporters. "This makes me feel like four years of training and sweating were worth nothing."

I don't want to trivialize Khakhaleichvili's experience. I'm sure it was heartbreaking for him. Athletics in his part of the world have ramifications far beyond what they are for most people in North America. A second gold medal could well have guaranteed Khakhaleichvili a lifetime of employment coaching judo in his Eastern European homeland. But I believe what happened to this Olympic athlete provides a valuable lesson about the "martial" aspect of a martial way.

When we think about the ancient Japanese samurai warriors, we are apt to picture them fighting. That is the way they are portrayed in woodblock prints and in movies—swords swinging as they leap furiously into battle and engage in feats of great courage and physical prowess. Although the samurai undoubtedly did participate in such adventures from time to time, sword fights were rarely their major problem in combat.

In 1587, for example, the Japanese warlord Hideyoshi Toyotomi embarked on a campaign to subdue Kyushu, the southernmost island of Japan, which was under the rule of the powerful Shimazu samurai family. It was a tremendous undertaking, and Hideyoshi raised an army of 200,000 men for the job. He invaded Kyushu and pushed the Shimazu clan into retreat. The Shimazu, however, were not about to give up their homeland without a struggle, and they fought back, causing Hideyoshi's invasion to suffer the hot and rainy Kyushu summer climate.

Because of the constant rain, Hideyoshi's troops were never able to dry out their clothing or armor, and they soon developed skin infections. Crotches and underarms became chafed and blistered so badly they bled. Soon, many of Hideyoshi's men could not walk or even move their arms effectively. In the end, the Shimazu surrendered the island—just five days before Hideyoshi had secretly set a date for withdrawing and giving up the invasion. His campaign proved successful, but just barely. Hideyoshi was nearly defeated by what we would refer to today as severe jock itch and diaper rash.

Another great samurai general, Kato Kiyomasa, lost a battle early in his career when the entire stock of rations he brought for his troops became infested with maggots.

Takeda Shingen, who went on to become one of Japan's renowned military leaders, nearly lost a battle owing to a single rainstorm. He had to frantically change his attack plans when the rain ruined the leather head of a huge drum used for relaying information to his field commanders. The drum was soaked and wouldn't play loudly enough to be heard.

The fact is, when we're talking about things that are "martial," we can't limit ourselves merely to battlefield heroics or tactics. If you can't get to the battlefield, if you're too sick or sore or hungry to fight once you get there, if you can't communicate effectively with your teammates, it probably won't matter how skilled you are or how long you've trained.

Ask anyone who has gone to Japan to pursue *budo* training, and he'll tell you that the actual training was rarely the biggest challenge he faced. He also had to contend with the unusual food, not to mention the matter of transportation. (If Khakhaleichvili thinks public transportation was complicated in Atlanta, he ought to take a look at a subway map of Tokyo.) It is not unusual for foreign martial artists to travel two hours or more to get to their *dojo*, with train changes along the way.

Bravery, skill and tactics all play a part in attaining victory. But as Kiyomasa, Shingen and Hideyoshi could tell you, other less-tangible factors also come into play. The technical logistics of battle are equally as important as what happens once you're in the fight itself.

Khakhaleichvili learned this lesson in an agonizing way. He lost a chance to prove his judo skills before the entire world, against the best in the world. On the other hand, he should take some comfort in knowing that he is in the company of some very great warriors who, in their own ways, also experienced glitches in making it to the competition.

# LESSONS IN PAIN

*February 1997*

If you are a karate practitioner, you need to make friends with someone who practices *aikido*. You need to do this because aikido techniques can teach karate practitioners some very valuable lessons about managing pain. I'm sure a lot of karate practitioners believe they are qualified to write an entire book on the subject of pain. Any longtime practitioner whose karate training is even halfway serious has likely absorbed his share of bruises and contusions, sprained joints, and a host of other physical misfortunes that come with hard practice.

If you think about it, however, chances are that most of the pain you have suffered came suddenly, unexpectedly. You accidentally stopped a reverse punch with your nose. You went one-on-one with the *makiwara* and discovered that your wrist wasn't up to the task. You tried to throw a roundhouse kick to someone's head and your hip exploded. We've all been there.

Traditional karate, by and large, does not include the kind of pain that can be inflicted slowly and deliberately, in gradually increasing degrees.

---

**While you can learn to escape wrestling and other holds by perfecting countermeasures and using your strength and flexibility, to compete effectively against pain, you must develop a mentality that can deal with its effects without surrendering control of your body and your means of defense.**

---

Aikido, on the other hand, specializes in this sort of pain.

I recommend that karate practitioners go to an aikido school either before classes begin or after they're over. Ask the instructor to teach you some of the basic aikido pinning techniques that inflict pain. *Nikkyo* is a good one; *sankyo* is even better. These are sophisticated techniques, and you won't learn all of their subtleties in a short time. At first, you want the ability to execute these immobilization techniques on a partner who is going along willingly with the movement.

I have seen very skilled martial artists have these techniques used on them for the first time, and it is a remarkable sight. They go from being skeptics to believers in the time it takes to have their wrists captured and

controlled—about half a second. What is most interesting about their reaction is how uncontrolled it is. These same martial artists might, during sparring sessions, absorb a punch to the mouth that splits a lip and leaves them bleeding profusely, yet they will barely react to the pain because they are accustomed to it. The pain of a wrist lock, however, is entirely foreign to them, and they respond quite dramatically and without any sense of self-control.

With time and practice, your reaction to these kinds of joint locks will become much less immediate. You will begin to see that pain, especially when you know it is coming, is something over which you have some control. You can learn to compartmentalize it and accept it without allowing it to absorb your entire attention.

But the first time you're placed in a good wrist lock, you'll be thinking about nothing but the pain, which at this initial stage of training will have almost complete control over your body. You might collapse in a heap on the floor. Some beginners have actually wet their pants when locks of this nature have been applied—dramatic and embarrassing proof of just how much control can be surrendered.

Unlike aikido, Western forms of grappling, such as wrestling, generally seek to control an opponent's body by immobilizing it. Pain is not an issue. If you are pinned to the ground and denied effective use of your limbs, you can no longer mount an offense. The bulk of judo grappling techniques provide the same result.

Holds that emphasize pain, however, are designed to immobilize an opponent by distracting him with so much discomfort that he is unable to launch an attack. And while you can learn to escape wrestling and other holds by perfecting countermeasures and using your strength and flexibility, to compete effectively against pain, you must develop a mentality that can deal with its effects without surrendering control of your body and your means of defense. Learning some of the basic aikido locks and holds is an excellent way to begin this process, and it's a step that should be taken by every serious martial artist.

# THE GATEWAY TO THE MARTIAL PATH
*March 1997*

Some time ago, I took part in a martial arts demonstration, and when I had finished, a few people came up to me to ask questions. One of them, trying to get my attention, said, "Excuse me, *sensei.*"

Reflexively, I responded, "I'm not a sensei." What he said next truly shocked me.

"*Shihan?*" he asked.

For an instant, I was tempted to laugh, and then to my horror, I saw he was serious. "Shihan" is one of many terms used to describe (but almost never to personally address) a karate master. This person actually thought I'd been insulted by being referred to merely as a teacher and assumed I wanted to be recognized as a master.

I explained to him that, not only was I not a shihan, I wasn't yet at the skill level at which I could even be considered a teacher. I told him I could probably best be described as a *nyumonsha*—a beginner.

The word "nyumonsha" is actually not used much in modern Japanese. Tragically, it is used even less in the United States, where, in terms of the martial disciplines, it should be used frequently. The last character *sha* refers to a person who does something—a practitioner. The *nyu* at the

---

**If we're serious about our journey along the "martial path," we must always think of ourselves as *nyumonsha*.**

---

beginning of the word is written with the same strokes that are sometimes pronounced *irimi*, meaning "to enter." A *mon* is a gate. Putting the entire word together, we have "a person entering the gate."

To gain a truer understanding of "entering the gate," we must take into consideration the traditional Japanese approach to architecture. Like so many things in Japan, architecture has been influenced by the threat of warfare. The civil war in Japan lasted more than two centuries. People had to adapt to living in a country that was essentially a war zone, and you can still see some of the methods they used in the way a traditional Japanese home is built: Although the houses are square, the rooms inside are often arranged in a spiral pattern.

You find this design in Japanese castles, as well. You enter through one gate, but to gain access to the innermost recesses of the structure, you have to go around and around, through a series of openings—more "gates"—until you reach your destination. Most people visiting a Japanese home or castle had no need to penetrate that far; their business could usually be conducted in one of the outer rooms. Only members of the family or those who were very trusted would have reason to advance into the *okunoma*—the "hidden spaces"—at the heart of the structure.

In castle architecture, you can see why such an arrangement would be strategically sound. An invading force could easily wear themselves out, constantly turning corners as they sought to penetrate the defenses, and at every turn they would be under attack.

Strangely, similar labyrinths exist in Japanese buildings that were never threatened by enemy forces. A typical Shinto shrine, for instance, is built in this same pattern. The innermost precinct of a shrine is always at the center of a group of encircling rooms or buildings. A Japanese teahouse is similarly situated, wrapped inside an outer and then an inner garden constructed to contain it. So perhaps this spiral formation has deeper roots in the Japanese psyche than can be found in the necessities of warfare.

Whatever the reason for such architecture, we can see that a "person at the gate" is someone who has a lot of work ahead of him. He has no direct path to the heart of things. He has to go around and around, approaching his destination obliquely. That's why, if we're serious about our journey along the "martial path," we must always think of ourselves as nyumonsha. There is always another gate before us, another turn, another new discovery to be made.

# THERE'S NO ROOM FOR BRUTALITY IN THE MARTIAL ARTS

*May 1997*

I followed my instructor's command and delivered a front kick to his midsection. He slipped past my oncoming foot, swept it with his forearm and tossed me to the ground of the old cemetery where we were practicing. I jumped back up as quickly as I could.

"Again!" he shouted.

I faked a step-in punch, then shuffled forward and unleashed a reverse punch. My instructor didn't fall for the fake; he slid his arm down my punching arm, let it come right up against my neck, and tossed me back in a kind of clothesline throw similar to *aikido's irimi nage*. I went down again—hard.

My next attack was another front kick, which I pulled back too quickly for my instructor to grab. Then I kicked again with my rear leg. He was too close to block effectively; for a second, I thought I had him. But he leaped into the air, tucking his legs and twisting around so the kick just missed him, and he punched me on the chin just hard enough to force me off-balance and knock me down again.

---

**Whether dealing with children or adults, the line separating hard training from brutal training is clearly crossed when a student is deliberately humiliated, especially in the presence of others.**

---

And so it went. I attacked until I was too exhausted to put up much of a fight, and my teacher countered each time and threw me to the ground. When we finished the lesson, I had more of the cemetery dirt on my uniform than some of the graves around me had over them. I could taste blood where one of my instructor's punches had cut the inside of my lip. And I had a lot of bruises and scrapes, as well as a sprained finger—the result of an ill-fated knifehand strike that he had grabbed and turned into a finger lock. I was, at the end of that and many other lessons, a sore puppy.

But was I brutalized?

This is a serious question. When exactly does training go beyond the bounds of hard practice and into the realm of brutality? When is a teacher simply being rough with students as a part of normal training, and when is he being vicious? It's a fine line, for sure.

Like most practitioners who practice one of the traditional martial ways for a long time, I have experienced my share of harsh practices, some of which could have been interpreted as cruel. When I was in high school, training with a university judo club, the students went on barefoot runs around the campus in the dead of winter over icy, snow-covered pavement. We accepted this as a part of training. I remember a football coach telling my judo teacher that, if he asked his players to do such a thing, he'd probably be fired. But in judo, this sort of training was common—and still is—all over the world.

Were we *judoka* being brutalized by having to run barefoot in the snow? It is a difficult question to answer. I know for certain that brutality plays a role—too large a role—in much of *budo* practice.

When it comes to children, there is never any excuse to employ force. If, for example, a child is too scared to execute a forward roll in an aikido class, he should never be forced to. The teacher should take the child aside and work with him, or assign a senior to do it. If the child simply cannot do something that is vital to his progress in a martial art—one must be able to roll in aikido or judo, for example—the parents should be advised and they should decide whether to keep their son or daughter enrolled.

Whether dealing with children or adults, the line separating hard training from brutal training is clearly crossed when a student is deliberately humiliated, especially in the presence of others. "Deliberate" is the key word here. Let's say, for instance, that your judo class is going on one of those winter runs, and you decide your health is not up to it and elect to stay in the *dojo*. That is your choice, and no one taunts you or tries to talk you into it. In this case, if you are embarrassed or humiliated by remaining behind, it cannot be blamed on the instructor or the rest of the class. But if you are punished, ostracized or otherwise mistreated because of your failure to participate in the run, it is an example of brutality.

Most instances of brutality are not so easily defined. There are, however, some preventative measures that can be taken to minimize your chances of experiencing such an incident. It is, for example, a good idea to watch an instructor's class before signing up for lessons.

Obviously, someone who has never seen an aikido class—in which bodies are regularly flying through the air and slamming to the mat—will, in a heartbeat, say that such training is brutal. And a beginner in a karate class who is asked to punch 100 times will wake up the next morning sore and stiff, and he will be tempted to conclude that it was an unusually tough

THE BEST OF DAVE LOWRY

workout. But we who have more experience in the budo know that these are just normal classes.

Consider the following questions when watching a martial arts class. Even if the instructor is pushing the students hard, does he still seem to have an interest in their safety? Does he humiliate them as part of their training? Do the students seem to be fearful or, worse, to be "zombies"? Do you see a lot of students with injuries, bandages, limps or the like? If there is rigorous training, is there some kind of "cool-down" process before class ends that reduces the level of aggression? Do the students look like people with whom you'd like to associate outside of training? Mature, well-balanced individuals do not, as a whole, remain in situations in which brutality is involved. The composition of the class very often reflects the character of the teacher.

Brutality is a subject all martial arts practitioners and teachers should think and talk about. It is every bit as important as how to perform a front kick or reverse punch correctly. The warrior way includes many aspects of physical and psychological training, but unnecessary violence should not be one of them.

# "SEALING" THE TECHNIQUE

June 1997

I had a judo teacher who often spoke of "sealing" a martial arts technique. He was referring to the subtle action performed during the crucial stage of executing a technique that guarantees its successful completion. This concept of sealing a technique really hit home in my own training, and I began to think about how I could apply it in practice.

I gradually found places in my karate training where it seemed that barely noticeable "tricks" were at work which ensured that my kick, punch or strike would be successful. That's not to say the techniques would not work without these little adjustments, but attacks and blocks were sealed with their addition.

Some students employ one or two of these sealing actions, while advanced practitioners use four or five in a single technique. Often the moves were so subtle that one would need to watch the technique repeatedly before noticing them.

One example of sealing occurs when an opponent delivers a midlevel punch, which you evade and follow up by seizing his elbow sleeve and executing a foot sweep. Your concentration tends to be on your feet and legs as you try to make solid contact with the opponent's ankle. That means

---

When you practice sealing a technique, make a habit of pausing after your final attack and consider your posture and your position in relation to launching another attack.

---

your grip on his sleeve could be loose and not contributing to the throw. The sweep often still works, but the opponent has his arm free and is able to use it to prop himself up before falling. His balance and posture are not completely broken, and he can recover and use his legs to kick you. One of the sealing actions for this technique is to hold the opponent's elbow tightly and pull it in a circular motion as you execute the sweep. The opponent is thus denied the use of the arm closest to the ground as he goes down, and he has no chance to catch himself and launch a counterattack.

Another example of sealing occurs when executing a right-leg side kick, followed by a right roundhouse kick. After repeating these techniques a few times, notice where your arms are at the kicks' crucial moment. Start with your rear (left) arm. When executing both the side and roundhouse kicks, this arm tends to drift out and away from the trunk. This dangling rear arm is a typical sight in beginning karate classes, used as a counterweight to help the practitioner maintain his balance, but experienced practitioners sometimes do it, too. The front (right) arm is often pulled back as well, causing the right fist to end up somewhere in the vicinity of your buttocks as the kick connects with its target.

You can still kick effectively with your arms in these positions, far from your body and swinging wildly. But if you seal them and keep them connected to the center of your body, tensing your underarms, you will find that the front arm is in a position to deliver a follow-up jab, while the rear arm will be situated so you can execute an immediate reverse punch. In this case, the position of the arms is a sealing action that improves the kinesiology of the kicks, but it also allows for an immediate follow-up strike should the kick fail to do the damage you wish.

An exercise that was devised by Yasuyuki Aragane of the Japan Karate Association illustrates how important the arms can be in sealing a technique after a kick. The exercise is a form of one-step sparring. As your opponent delivers an initial attack—in this case, a punch to your face—instead of blocking with your hands and arms, block the attack with a rising side kick.

This is a relatively dangerous exercise, intended for more advanced martial artists who can maintain their balance and control when kicking high. The idea is not to actually block the technique with force but rather to develop the timing, speed and flexibility to redirect the punch with your foot. Be careful during this drill, because a hard side kick to your partner's wrist or forearm can easily break bones. This exercise demonstrates how important your hands are in kicking. If you block the opponent's punch with your kick, you must immediately recover and either attack or seize your opponent. Either way, you will need to have perfect control over your arms.

Sealing is obviously a technique designed for more experienced practitioners. When you practice sealing a technique, make a habit of pausing after your final attack and consider your posture and your position in relation to launching another attack. In other words, have you sealed the last technique? This is a question that can only be answered through lengthy training.

# THE THREE BASIC CONCEPTS OF THE "WARRIOR WAYS"

*July 1997*

It is very popular in the martial arts community to compare the various Japanese *budo* to examine how each system would react to a similar attack or self-defense situation. This sort of analysis can provide a lot of information about the dynamics of these arts and can reveal the distinctions that separate them. If you oversimplify, however, and say, "Well, a karate practitioner does this, a judo player does that," you run the risk of overlooking some of the vital fundamentals that all of the budo have in common.

The fact is that the budo of Japan have basic concepts in common. They are not completely disparate arts, nor are they as different as some believe. Because they share a common origin (the martial disciplines of the samurai warrior) and a common ethnic and social root (Japan), there are bound to be links connecting karate with *kendo* and *aikido* with *kyudo*, even though all appear to have distinctly different approaches to fighting.

There are at least three basic concepts that form the foundation for all the Japanese martial ways. The first of these concepts is the emphasis on hip movement. This is a cornerstone of all Japanese martial arts. All movements originate with power derived from the hips. This is not always

---

In the Japanese *budo*, it doesn't matter whether you're executing a reverse punch, a strike with a *kendo shinai* or an *aikido* throw, you start the movement from your hips.

---

so with other combat arts in Asia, and it's obviously not true in Western fighting arts like boxing, in which power often comes from the shoulders. But in the Japanese budo, it doesn't matter whether you're executing a reverse punch, a strike with a kendo *shinai* or an aikido throw, you start the movement from your hips.

Why is it that the hips were chosen as the focal point for all the budo? One theory is that Japan has always been primarily an agricultural society, with rice being the biggest crop, so a lot of the people were accustomed to squatting and bending to tend to the rice—a grain that doesn't grow much taller than the knees. They would have naturally developed strong hips from working like this all the time. Another theory is that Japan was a place where people sat on the floor, and thus the people naturally developed a lower center of balance than might be found in other cultures. Of course, the most practical reason for the use of hip power has to do with the size of the muscles in the lower hips and thighs; they are the largest muscles in the human body, and making them the basis for movement of any kind, combative or otherwise, is a way to guarantee strength.

The second concept linking the various budo has to do with the focus of power. Think of the wide, swinging kicks found in some Korean methods of fighting. The ax kick, during which the practitioner's leg shoots up and then cuts down, landing on the opponent, is one example, as is the spinning back kick. Both of these kicks are foreign to Japanese and Okinawan karate. They are not included in the Japanese martial arts curriculum because they do not have a single, unified sense of focus. They instead have more of a reaping movement, cutting down whatever comes within the arc they create. Kicks in Japanese and Okinawan karate, on the other hand, always focus energy on an exact spot. This kind of focus is referred to in the Japanese fighting arts as *kime* or *tsume*.

The last concept that unifies all of the Japanese budo is that form always precedes function. Form, or *kata*, is the most vital method of transmitting or learning a skill in the budo. By kata, I mean the preset form—the correct way of doing something, from bowing to fastening one's belt knot. There is spontaneity in the martial ways, but it comes at the end of the process of the kata, as odd as this may sound to the uninitiated. You may agree with this method of learning, or you may not, but it is fundamental to all Japanese martial arts.

# RANK DOESN'T NECESSARILY HAVE ITS PRIVILEGES
*October 1997*

Tired of the politics and infighting taking place in their karate organization, a group of students quit the association to train on their own. Led
by a friend of mine, the group began meeting regularly at a high-school
gymnasium, where they conducted training sessions.

As the senior student in the group, my friend led the classes but never
considered himself a *sensei*. He did not award belt promotions or charge
for his instruction. The training was very informal, and it worked very well.
Each participant had connections with other karate schools or teachers
from their past, and each attended seminars and visited other schools to
contribute new ideas to the practice sessions.

But these individuals were not entirely happy with their new training
situation. They knew they needed regular instruction from one source, but
they were not willing to pay the price of being caught up in the politics of
a large organization.

One day, my friend received a phone call from someone who claimed
to be a *godan* (fifth-degree black belt) and had been living and training in
Japan for the past 15 years. The man said he was seriously considering
moving to my friend's city and opening a karate school. He had heard of
my friend's group and wanted to come to one of the practices. The tone

---

**A person's rank was once at least some indication of the
caliber of his character. Sadly, that is no longer the case.**

---

of the conversation left little doubt in my friend's mind that this man was
expecting the group to form the nucleus for his new school.

My friend had never heard of this person, but reasoned that, if he really
were a godan, his teaching would be a remarkable opportunity for the
group; godan-level instructors are scarce outside of Japan. On the other
hand, the karate group faced a dilemma. If they went along with the man's
plans and turned their club over to him, they would risk becoming involved
with an instructor whose personal character they knew nothing about. If
they refused to let him take over their group, they were risking passing up
a chance for a level of teaching that they might never have again.

My friend decided to invite the man to lead their next session. After
the class was over, he spoke privately with the man and told him that the

group wished him the best of luck in starting a new school. He volunteered some of his time if the godan needed help building or renovating a place, and he said the group would like to occasionally train at the new school, with the godan's permission. If the group had a chance to get to know him personally and got along with him, it might consider joining his school in the future. But, my friend said, for the time being, they were not interested in turning the club over to him.

It turned out that the godan quickly disappeared from the city and hasn't been heard from since. Maybe he was merely testing the waters and hoping to get a ready-made student enrollment. My friend and his group still wonder whether they did the right thing. I think they did.

In years past, if someone of godan level surfaced who had trained for a lengthy period in Japan, it was almost guaranteed that he was a person of character and someone you could trust. Back when fewer people were involved in the martial arts, it was difficult for someone to advance very far if he had questionable character. The system tended to weed most of them out. But today, there are numerous tales of people who went to Japan and trained for several years, were given high promotions and, on returning to teach in America, physically abused their students or took advantage of them sexually. A person's rank was once at least some indication of the caliber of his character. Sadly, that is no longer the case.

Today, if someone of high rank comes to a school uninvited, he should be treated like a visitor, and he should expect to be treated as such. He should not expect to teach a class, and no one should assume that his rank is indicative of his character. Even though he may technically be the senior, he does not have the right to come in and tell the school's owner how classes ought to be taught, how business should be conducted, or anything else. His advice might be valuable, but it is not mandatory for the school owner to follow it, and instructors should not allow such individuals to intimidate them. If these interlopers are good teachers and are truly who they claim to be, they will be able to open a school of their own.

If you like what you see in one of these senior instructors, then by all means ask to become a student. If not, keep on doing what you believe is right. That's what my friend did, and his group is much better off for it.

## CAN RANK BE TAKEN AWAY?

*April 1998*

Not long ago, a reader wrote to tell me a sad story. After many years of training in a particular karate school, he became disillusioned with the teacher and discontinued his practice there. In response, the teacher acted threatening and unpleasant. He demanded the return of the student's rank certificate and black belt. The student asked me how the Japanese martial artists of old would have handled such a situation and what I thought of the practice of asking a student or former student to surrender his rank and certificate.

Before answering, I must remind readers that the business of issuing belt ranks is less than a century old. According to most accounts, it was in the early part of the 20th century that judo-founder Jigoro Kano informally handed out lengths of black cotton belting to his senior students. Thus was born the concept of using colored belts to indicate rank. Asking how the Japanese martial artists of old would have reacted to a demand that their colored belts be returned after a disagreement is like asking how they would have handled a computer problem.

Ranks in the martial arts of the feudal period were of the *menkyo*, or "license," variety. Different traditions had different approaches. In some

---

**Frankly, I've always had a problem with teachers who demand a rank be returned after a student misbehaves in some way.**

---

schools, a single rank or document might be given to certify that the bearer was authorized to teach the art. Other schools used rankings in which a student held a certificate called a *go-mokuroku* or *sho-mokuroku*. This indicated that he had been indoctrinated into the "bottom half" (*go*) or "top half" (*sho*) of the "catalogue" (*mokuroku*) of techniques taught in the school. Aside from being an official teaching authorization, these documents were not very important in the overall scheme. If a student had fought in several battles and still had all his limbs, that alone would be a powerful testament to his skill. He didn't need a colored belt to prove anything.

The modern era's martial ways, however, were not designed as much for combat as for teaching such things as morals, physical fitness and aesthetic values. And since they are taught to the masses instead of to professional warriors, belt ranks have become a way of encouraging practice and rewarding effort. There's nothing wrong with this, but it has caused a lot of problems for the martial ways. Let's say a student hasn't missed a practice session in 10 years. He's always on the floor trying his best. Unfortunately, his best is rather pathetic. He's just not well-coordinated. Should he be given a belt to reward him for his efforts or only for actual physical progress in the mastery of techniques?

Other questions include determining what the awarded rank represents. If I get a certificate for climbing to the top of Mount Everest, the issuing organization could subsequently revoke it, I suppose. But that wouldn't take away my accomplishment. A license to practice medicine could be revoked by the state, which would indicate the holder had done something wrong legally or ethically. But while the revocation would prevent the doctor from practicing medicine, it would not necessarily indicate that he was technically incompetent to do so in the future. A certificate giving me privileges at a health club could be revoked simply because I didn't pay my dues. However, *budo* organizations have never been able to decide whether their rankings are like the climbing certificate, the medical license or the heath-club certificate.

I cannot imagine any of my *sensei* asking me to return a rank. But if they did, would it mean I could no longer perform technically at the level at which they had certified me? Or would it mean I had done something to make me no longer "deserve" the rank? Frankly, I've always had a problem with teachers who demand a rank be returned after a student misbehaves in some way.

In a famous incident some time ago, an *aikido* student was forced to return his rank to his teacher after it was revealed that the student, a teacher himself, had molested and assaulted female students. This seems fair. But what does it say about the teacher who gave him that rank in the first place? Shouldn't that teacher have been obliged to return *his* rank to *his* teacher in recognition of his obvious inability to judge the character of one of his senior students?

The teacher who awards a rank should be clear about what he's awarding and certifying. If he gives me a rank to indicate that I can perform technically at a particular level, then his subsequent demand to return that rank doesn't make sense. I performed, he rated me, that's the end of it. If a rank carries other connotations, he should make that clear. "This rank is a symbol of your membership in good standing in our school," the teacher might say. If this is the case and I do something awful and the teacher no longer wants me in his school, then it would make sense for him to ask me to return the rank as a symbolic statement that I am no longer a member.

If the rank is a symbol of my teacher's faith in me *and* a certification of my character, but my later actions demonstrate I was not worthy of his faith, then it would be my responsibility to return the rank on my own. It should also be the teacher's responsibility to do some serious thinking about his ability to judge character in his students.

The average martial arts teacher probably regards rank as a combination of all these things. That's why there is much confusion about the matter of returning a rank when something goes wrong in the teacher/student relationship. In the case of the reader, the details of his teacher's actions leave little doubt in my mind that the reader did the right thing in leaving the school. He may regret having to surrender his hard-won certificate. But on the other hand, would he really want a certificate from a place where he didn't respect the teacher or the teaching?

A rank and belt can be taken away, but no one can take away a person's skills. If they have been legitimately earned, a belt or a piece of paper isn't going to matter much in comparison.

# THE ART OF DEFENDING AGAINST SURPRISE
*May 1998*

In the old days, Japanese swordsmen often referred to the "four sicknesses" to which a warrior was susceptible: surprise, worry, doubt and fear. Surprise and its meaning for modern martial artists will be discussed this month, and the others will follow in the June, July and August issues.

The serious *budoka* must never be taken by surprise. Although he might train eight hours a day and be a world champion, his mental attitude makes him susceptible to a sneak attack. Therefore, all his practice will have amounted to nothing. It is only natural that martial artists would consider *fuiuchi*, or "surprise," to be one of the most insidious "illnesses."

Classically, avoiding surprise is approached in two ways. First, a person must develop external vigilance, a steady maintenance of his guard against any possible threats. This can serve as a physical defense against surprise. Often exposed to frequent, unexpected peril, the samurai were masters of physical defense. If we believe the stories about them, they went to extraordinary lengths in exercising and perfecting this defense. During wartime, for instance, they would randomly jab a spear or sword up into the ceiling of an unfamiliar room, thinking that spies were lurking overhead. Fans of popular samurai movies will recognize this practice, for it's almost a cliché: A warrior will thrust his weapon through the ceiling, then go about his business. A few moments later, the camera will pan to the small hole the blade made in the ceiling as it begins to run with blood.

To protect themselves against surprise, the samurai adopted many such habits. Even after the days of feudal-era battles, my *sensei* kept a heavy wooden sword leaning against a corner of his toilet room. He followed the example of Takeda Shingen, a great general who was supposed to have done the same. This was done to prevent himself from ever being surprised while he was unarmed. In addition to this, my sensei never relaxed in his bath without a dagger within arm's reach. Other similarly experienced swordsmen would not sit with their back to a doorway; instead, they positioned themselves at an angle that allowed them a view of anyone entering. They would also give themselves ample room to draw their weapon, if needed. They took equal precautions outside, carefully tilting their wide-brimmed straw hat down slightly to keep the sun's glare at a minimum and to prevent an opponent from knowing where their gaze was directed.

While probably not as drastic, modern martial artists often acquire similar habits. They check the rear seat of their cars before getting in, and while walking, they swing wide around street corners to preclude the possibility of an unexpected assault. However, like the samurai, modern-day martial artists using a purely physical approach to defense are soon confronted with a problem. After all, a guy's got to sleep, eat and brush his teeth. It's pretty tough to execute a side kick while taking a nap, or a reverse punch while eating a bowl of chili. No human being can be physically on-guard 24 hours a day.

This is where the second method of defending surprise enters the picture. Sometimes it's called *zanshin*, and while it is not entirely an accurate term to use, we shall do so here for the purposes of explanation.

Zanshin, which literally means "lingering mind," could be considered the spiritual counterpart to physical defense. It is best illustrated by a story handed down through generations of martial arts practitioners. There are many versions of it, and what follows is one of them.

A young man wished to learn the art of the sword, so he traveled to a region of mountains in the province of Kii that was threaded with 48 spectacular waterfalls. Cascading more than 400 feet, the tallest and most scenic of these was Nachi Falls. At the foot of it stood the Kumano shrine, which had been the site of ancient and mysterious rituals since time began. Behind the shrine lived a master swordsman.

After a long journey, the boy reached the Kumano shrine and found the master living in a hut nearby. "I've come to learn swordsmanship," the boy announced. "How long will it take me?"

"Ten years," the old master replied.

"That's too long," the boy said. "How about if I work extra hard and practice twice as much?"

"Twenty years," the master answered.

The boy saw that this conversation was leading nowhere, so he wisely argued no further. He simply requested that he be accepted as a student, and the master agreed.

It was a peculiar apprenticeship. The boy was put to work cutting firewood, cooking and cleaning up around the hut—chores that lasted from before dawn until after dark. The master rarely spoke, never mentioning swordsmanship to the boy. Finally, after a year of toil, the boy grew frustrated, suspecting he had been tricked into becoming nothing more than the master's unpaid servant.

While angrily chopping a log one day, the boy decided to find instruction elsewhere. Suddenly, he was sent reeling by a terrific blow. He looked up from the ground, dazed, only to find the master standing above him

brandishing a green bamboo stick. The master left as silently as he had come. But an hour later, while the boy was washing clothes near the falls, the old man struck again, harder this time, and he roared over the crashing of the waterfall: "You expect to learn swordsmanship, yet you can't even dodge a simple hit from a stick!"

The boy's pride was understandably wounded. He resolved to stay with the master and prove him wrong. He began to concentrate on keeping his mind clear and receptive to an attack, and while he suffered many more strikes in the following months, he was able to anticipate some of them and effectively ward them off. When the master's slashing blows started to come at night, he learned to sleep lightly; his subconscious stayed alert to every sound. The more successful the youth grew at avoiding the bamboo stick, the more frequently the attacks became. Dozens of times a day, the master would suddenly be there, swinging at him. The youth's instincts sharpened, and as the months went by it became more and more difficult for the master to catch him unaware.

Three years after he had come to the Kumano shrine, the boy was nearly a man. One night, while he was totally absorbed preparing dinner, the master struck from behind. But now, the young man's spirit was so well-disciplined that he merely fended off the blow with a pot lid and returned to his cooking without a pause. That night, the master presented his student with a fine old sword and wrote out a certificate of full mastery. The young man did not need either, though. Without ever having a formal lesson, he had become a man of phenomenal martial powers.

We don't know what happened to the master's student, or even if the story is true. But if it is, one thing is certain—the young man who learned his art at the foot of Nachi Falls was never, ever, taken by surprise.

# THE ART OF COPING WITH WORRY
*June 1998*

Outside the house, crickets were chirping under the last full moon of the summer. Inside, I lay awake in the small hours of the morning, kicking at the covers and tossing fitfully. I wasn't in a mood to listen to the concert of the insects. I was too worried, as most of us are from time to time, about money. The kitchen sink was clogged again, which meant yet another expensive visit from the plumber. The phone bill was exorbitant, and the car had just come down with a case of the clattering squeaks.

Relatively inexpensive worries these financial concerns were, but as worries often do when they come late at night, they festered and nagged. It wasn't long before I was worrying about all kinds of things. Was there enough money in our savings in case of some disaster? Would my income as a writer ever be sufficient for us to live as we wished? By this time, I was totally absorbed by my anxieties. I sat up in frustration. My gaze fell on the polished length of an old wooden practice sword—a *bokken* that was sitting on its rack in the corner. It gleamed in the moonlight.

Years earlier, when neither my bokken nor I was quite so battered, I'd held it across my knees one night after training with my *sensei*, listening

---

**The legendary swordsman Miyamoto Musashi once commented that few people are defeated in life by a single, overwhelming crisis.**

---

to him tell a story about Ota Toshihiro. Ota was an expert in the *kagami ryu*. He lived in Japan during an age when swordsmen often dueled for no better reason than to prove the superiority of their skills with the blade.

Ota lived in Nara, and one day he was approached by three young fencers from nearby Kyoto. The youths were doing what might be called *dojo arashi*, literally "dojo storming." They would visit different martial artists in different dojo and ask for "instruction," which was merely a veiled request for a duel. It was a way of learning and a way of establishing one's reputation as a fighter. The three had heard of Ota, and they'd come to him to fight. Ota, irritated by their rudeness, explained that he hadn't the time to give lessons to every stumblebum who happened along. Angry at the snub, the three turned their request into a demand. Knowing he'd have to face them eventually, Ota agreed to a match the following day.

The young swordsmen were talented, but Ota was a veteran of these sorts of encounters. When he met them the following morning, he drew his weapon and cut off the hand of one of the challengers before the man could even unsheathe his sword. The other two attacked. Ota killed them both.

In relating this tale, my sensei didn't concentrate on any details of the fight. Instead, he asked me a question about the incident: "How do you suppose Ota felt the night before that duel?"

The question was a good one. It is one that could be asked about any of the martial artists of that time who constantly risked death or dishonor in traveling the way of the warrior. Think about it. One moment that afternoon in long-ago Japan, Ota was enjoying his day and going about his business. The next minute, he faced the likelihood that this was his last afternoon on earth, that he might die the very next day. To adapt himself to that kind of lifestyle and learn to control his emotions during those long hours of darkness before the duel, Ota must have cultivated extraordinary mental fortitude. He must have developed a very good perspective on personal problems. With death always in mind, worries about a leaking roof, for instance, or a minor spat with a neighbor must have become terribly insignificant.

Today, of course, we don't have a lifestyle like Ota's. We don't live in a world at all like his. Rarely, if ever, do we put our skills to the ultimate test. But if a serious martial artist is to recognize life's difficulties and annoyances in a realistic way, his attitude must be similar in some ways to Ota's. Just as we imagine Ota might have done, the martial artist must take notice of the leaky roof, arrange to have it repaired and attend to life's other problems and annoyances. Yet they will never distract him from his greater goals: to become a better person, to appreciate what life gives him and to meet his responsibilities to others.

The legendary swordsman Miyamoto Musashi once commented that few people are defeated in life by a single, overwhelming crisis. Some of us might experience disasters, such as losing both our parents while we're young or having our home and savings wiped out by a natural disaster. But more often, as Musashi noted, people are beaten down by a series of minor distractions or difficulties that pile up.

Musashi would have recognized Shakespeare's complaint that, when troubles come, "they come not as single spies but in battalions." They gradually take their toll on us. We experience this in the dojo just as we do in everyday life. A pulled muscle one week results in a disappointing demonstration of *kata* at a tournament the next week. And then the car breaks down, and we have no way to get to the dojo to train the week after that. These are the sorts of annoyances that can pile up, just as unexpected expenses, social obligations and the strain of limited finances can.

A practitioner of a martial way must put these impediments in their place—while giving them the attention they need, of course. But he must never permit them to distract him from the aims of all *budo* training: the refinement of his art and his self.

Remember the example set by Ota and all the dedicated martial artists who came before us. I did. Then I shelved my worries that night and eventually fell asleep. In the warm summer night, the crickets sang on, and my old bokken continued to shine in the moonlight.

# THE ART OF DEALING WITH DOUBT

*July 1998*

It was a late summer afternoon in the ninth year of *Keicho* (1605 by the Western calendar), and the fine, dusty haze hung so heavily over the countryside that the servant boy, slouched against a pillar on the veranda of the *dojo*, did not even see the traveler at first. The stranger appeared slowly, distorted by the haze and heat, looking more like a quivering shadow floating down the dirt road without substance. As he drew closer, though, he assumed a form that was all too familiar, one often seen trudging the roads of early Tokugawa-era Japan. In a country that had just been torn apart by war, the roads were filled with homeless itinerants. The figure approaching the dojo did not seem exceptional. Still, there was a determination apparent in his stride, a sense of urgency in the way he carried himself, so the servant boy stood to receive him as he came through the gate.

"Is this the training hall of Yoshihira Fukui?" the stranger asked.

The boy nodded.

"Please tell Fukui *sensei* that I would like him to face me in a match of skill with any weapon of his choice."

Again the boy nodded, then led the stranger to a foyer of the dojo to wait. He raced off to tell his master of the challenge.

Fukui was an expert teacher of the *shinto-ryu* of martial arts and was considered to be a fine technician of the school. He enjoyed the benefits of

---

**[Fukui] realized that all the terrors he'd experienced about the duel had come not from any reality but from his own mind.**

---

employment from a wealthy *daimyo* and was responsible for teaching the martial arts to every samurai in the daimyo's forces. Yet like every martial arts teacher, Fukui was subject to a certain occupational hazard.

It was a custom of the time for warriors to travel around, visiting the training halls of various teachers and making challenges. Teachers could refuse, of course, and sometimes they were actually forbidden by their employing lords to engage in such duels. But too many refusals could result in a loss of reputation. Conversely, if the teacher was too careless in jumping in to fight every challenger who happened along, he risked being killed or disgraced. It was a no-win situation for the teacher: Lose, and he could die or appear incompetent; win, and his only reward was defeating someone who was, after all, simply a wandering nobody.

For this reason, Fukui disliked such duels, and he growled at his servant boy: "See that the stranger is well-fed, and tell him I'll meet him in the practice yard in two hours."

With a belly full of hot rice and pickled vegetables, the stranger did not look so wild or intimidating. In fact, waiting under the eaves of the dojo, he reminded Fukui—who was watching him unobserved from above—of the nervous merchants who always appeared at the castle to plead for tax exemptions for this reason or that. Fukui smiled. The stranger's sword hung loosely from his belt, not tucked up tightly the way a professional swordsman would wear it. His whole bearing was one of unguarded sloppiness. "I could be on him before he knew it," Fukui thought, relieved.

Then, from nowhere, came a most disturbing notion. "What if his carelessness is an act?" Fukui thought. "He must know he's being watched right now. Maybe his manner is a trick meant to lure me into carelessness."

Fukui's doubts were not without some foundation. Many famous warriors were renowned for such trickery. Genshin Arima, for example, was said to look as if he were about to nap just before he fought a duel. Fukui's cheeks flushed. "What if ... What if ..." He felt sick to his stomach as he considered the possibility that he might be facing an eccentric master. He'd better get it over with, he decided, before his suspicions grew any worse.

The stranger scrambled to his feet when Fukui entered the practice yard. After exchanging names, both men drew their weapon. Fukui assumed the *itto-ryu's seigan* position with his sword extended in front of him, but he did not recognize the stance taken by his opponent. The man looked like he was holding a sword for the first time, in fact.

"What's he doing?" Fukui wondered. "That position has a score of gaps in it!"

But once again, he reconsidered his first impression: "Perhaps I was right earlier about this all being a trick. He could be luring me right into a trap. He must have some extraordinary confidence to walk into a duel with such nonchalance."

Perspiration beaded on Fukui's lip, and he felt another drop of it trickling down his spine. He started to take a step closer, but his legs suddenly would not carry him. His tongue was glued to the roof of his mouth. The situation was looking worse and worse, and for the first time Fukui thought he might be facing his own death.

After a long pause, Fukui's spirit was resolved. Determined to give a good account of himself, even if he died in the process, Fukui swung his sword up.

"Wait!" the stranger screamed, dropping his sword with a clatter. He fell to his knees beside it. Sobbing, he told his tale. He was no swordsman, he admitted. Instead, he was a simple traveling storyteller, an entertainer who'd found himself on the outskirts of town, empty of both pocket and stomach. He had heard that Fukui was the local martial arts teacher, so he decided to pass himself off as a swordsman, knowing it was customary for challenging fencers to be given a meal at the dojo where they had come to fight. He'd been so hungry that he hadn't considered the consequences of his imposture. Now he stopped talking and looked up, cowering, expecting Fukui to strike off his head at any second.

The storyteller was surprised to see the dojo master on the floor beside him. Gripping his sword, Fukui had, at that moment, experienced a kind of enlightenment. He realized that all the terrors he'd experienced about the duel had come not from any reality but from his own mind. All his training had crumbled in the face of self-defeating thoughts. The skills he'd acquired through years of practice were no match for a mind full of doubts. According to the scrolls of the school, Fukui's moment of realization marked the creation of the *munen-ryu*, the "no-thought tradition," of swordsmanship.

There is no way to overcome the illness of doubt, except through intensive training that strengthens the mind as well as the body. When a *budoka* has practiced so long and hard that his movements become automatic—without conscious thought—he will find that the doubts assailing him are no longer the problem they once were. In the words of a 14th-century Zen philosopher: "If your ears see and your eyes hear, you will harbor no doubts. How naturally the rain drips from the eaves!"

# THE ART OF OVERCOMING FEAR
*August 1998*

Possibly because it's an emotion closely related to our self-esteem, fear is a difficult concept to discuss in logical and unemotional terms. It's a sensation that springs from deep within us and emerges in the form of quivering knees, a churning stomach, sweating palms and throbbing temples. Libraries are filled with research to explain these reactions. Scholars speak of the animal behavior we've retained in our "fight or flight" tendencies, and scientific tests have been conducted to record our every physical response to fear.

But even without all that research, without being taped to electrodes and galvanic skin-response meters, we seem to know that fear is an illness that afflicts everyone. And as martial artists, we know its effects can be devastating.

Hearing stories of the *budoka* of old could lead us to believe that those people possessed some secret power that rendered them immune to the ravages of fear. They were not immune, of course. Most of the samurai of feudal Japan were really just well-conditioned to circumstances that appear fearful to us.

For professional warriors, this conditioning began very early in life. While they were still children, members of the samurai class were expected to conduct themselves with a kind of dignity that placed great emphasis on demonstrations of courage. They were frequently given tasks specifically designed to test their mettle. A 7- or 8-year-old boy might be instructed to deliver some message to distant relatives, leading him on a trip through forests or strange cities. Children were often sent on errands that required them to pass cemeteries or places rumored to be haunted. When they were not much older, they often witnessed the execution of criminals.

These are examples of child rearing that most of us would not endorse today. There is little doubt, too, that such practices had an effect on the psyche of these children that we would not find particularly healthy. To be fair, however, we must remember that those were different times. Only a generation or two ago in our own country, children regularly saw animals being slaughtered for cooking, and they even participated in the act. This is a chore most parents, including myself, would not readily assign their children today.

During the turbulent centuries of Japan's long civil wars, there weren't many young samurai who had not seen blood shed violently before they were out of their teenage years. In more than a few cases, they were responsible for the shedding. Numerous battalion commanders were no older than 16, and rigorous martial arts training was a regular part of their lives. Therefore, it is understandable that they were less disturbed by violent confrontations than many people might be today.

However, the assumption that apprehension and fear were not a concern for the samurai is decidedly inaccurate. Throughout their history, the samurai were very concerned with fear and its effects, as is revealed in the writings they left behind. For instance, the thoughts of Prince Otsu were recorded on the eve of his execution in the *Kaifuso* ("Poems of Tender Reminiscence"), a book compiled in 751. Otsu faced death for leading an ill-fated attempt to overthrow the government, and as his words indicate, he was frightened by what lay ahead:

> *The golden crow lights on the western roofs,*
> *Evening drums beat out the shortness of life,*
> *There are no inns on the highway to the grave,*
> *Into whose house will I enter tonight?*

In the early 18th century, a minor samurai named Tsunetomo Yamamoto took up the subject of fear in his famous treatise *Hagakure* ("Hidden Among the Leaves"):

> *The realization of certain death should be renewed every morning. Each morning you must prepare yourself for every kind of death. With composure of mind, imagine yourself broken by bows, guns, spears, swords, carried off by floods, leaping into a huge fire, struck by lightning, torn apart by earthquake, plunging from a cliff, as a disease-ridden corpse.*

Yamamoto and other samurai were wise enough to know that fear could never be entirely eliminated from the mind of a sane human being. Instead of trying to extinguish it, they sought ways to exploit the emotion, to use it to their own benefit. By concentrating daily on the greatest of mankind's fears—the fear of death—they knew that their apprehensions could be neutralized, then actually employed as a catalyst to energize the samurai so he was more effective in serving his lord.

Like Yamamoto and the other samurai of the feudal era, modern martial artists must recognize that fear can never be totally eliminated. Even veteran practitioners have known the unpleasant sensation of butterflies in their stomach and the jittery nerves of fear at one time or another. The most accomplished of them try not to ignore their fear but channel it productively. At an important event, job interview or public speech, the average person allows his fear to be directed in negative ways—in a squeaky,

## Yamamoto and other samurai were wise enough to know that fear could never be entirely eliminated from the mind of a sane human being.

quavering voice and nervous, distracted mannerisms, for instance. During a threatening situation, he tends to do the same, withdrawing into a world of indecisive, ineffectual actions.

The well-trained martial artist, on the other hand, responds to a stressful occasion by expressing his fear in a positive way, speaking confidently and allowing his apprehension to emerge in the form of a greater dignity and calmness. When directly threatened, whether in a sporting event or in real combat, his reaction to fear is expressed through the strength of his posture and the bold delivery of his technique.

As a budoka and as a person living in this danger-fraught, anxiety-ridden world, you cannot expect to escape fear. Escape isn't an option in our society. Fear is a standard feature. However, you do have a choice in how fear can show itself. It can be seen as an enemy to avoid or as a tool to help you through your training and your life.

68

# THE MILESTONE OF TURNING 42

*September 1998*

I'll be 42 next year. That's an age that doesn't mean much by Western standards—except that I now recognize none of the performers on MTV. In the West, certain ages are significant: 16, 21 and the dreaded 40. In Japanese culture, however, 42 is very significant.

In old Japan, certain ages were very important. At the age of 5, for example, boys from samurai families participated in ceremonies in which they were given wooden or dull metal swords to wear regularly for the first time. Even today in many of the traditional arts, a child's training begins at this age, specifically on the fifth day of the fifth month. At the age of 14, boys were given sets of real weapons, adult names and the responsibilities that went with their respective ranks.

The age of 42 is not as important as some of the others, but it has a meaning all its own—especially to exponents of the classical and some of the modern Japanese martial arts and ways. That's because 42 marks the year in a martial artist's life when he is expected to have matured in an important way.

In Japanese astrology, 12 animal signs are combined with 10 elements made up of wood, earth, fire, metal and water. These elements occur in

---

**[Age 42] is the time when you take your art from the realm of the purely physical into areas that have been previously closed to you because you lacked maturity or insight.**

---

"greater" and "lesser" fluctuations to equal 10. At the age of 42, a person has lived through all of the permutations of these signs (called *junishi* in Japanese) and elements *(jikkan)* twice.

The age of 42 also has a meaning in the older fighting arts of Japan. According to tradition, it is at this age that one's physical skills have reached their height. According to this way of looking at life, a person is unable to get much stronger or faster. With the nutrition and exercise methods of the modern day, we may be able to push that peak back a bit, but with the body's catabolic processes being what they are, I suspect the ancient Japanese were close to being on the mark with this observation. That's the downside of reaching 42.

The upside is that at 42 you're supposed to begin developing your mental powers to their fullest. At this age, you should have pretty much polished your techniques and built your strength and endurance. You need to begin perfecting the more subtle aspects of your training—things like timing, rhythm and setting up your opponent through psychological tricks. This is the time when you take your art from the realm of the purely physical into areas that have been previously closed to you because you lacked maturity or insight.

In Japanese, the phrase *yonju-ni sai* literally means "42 years old." But poetically, it is referred to as *fuwaku-ni*. *Fuwaku* means "40 years old" (literally, the word means "to put an end to confusion"). At 40, we're supposed to have matured to the point at which we can see the world and our place in it more clearly. We are no longer confused by the distractions of our hormones, by our fantasies, or by our worries and fears. So at two years beyond that, at fuwaku-ni, we are prepared to live in a more enlightened way. It is for this reason that many of the classical *koryu*, or martial arts of the feudal period, have rules that require a practitioner to have reached 42 before a license of full mastery—sometimes called *menkyo kaiden*—is granted.

This may be shocking to all the 20- and 30-year-olds out there who consider themselves masters. Many young people who seriously believe they are advanced masters do not understand the complexities of real *budo*. A serious martial way is composed of far more than simple technique. One might learn all the methods and *kata* of a style and still be considered a beginner. It is not until the mental and spiritual elements of the particular art are added that we can consider true growth to have been initiated. No matter how intelligent or skillful the practitioner, this mental element is one that can be developed only through time and experience in the *dojo* as well as in life. Depending on the kind of life and times in which we live, this can occur at different ages. But the masters of old realized that the insights necessary for perfecting an art usually started to come after one had lived about 40 years.

The age requirement for certain teaching licenses in the martial arts of old Japan was not a random decision on the part of the masters of the various schools. It's important to realize that what appears to be a simple superstition or folk belief might actually have very sophisticated and rational value. If you explain to many people that the age requirement of 42 is based on astrological computations, they might dismiss it as mumbo-jumbo. We often have to look behind the belief to see that people in earlier times were much smarter than we give them credit for.

What does all this mean for today's karate practitioner? First of all, because one must reach a certain age and maturity to understand many of the subtleties of the art, a person should not automatically believe that, just because he's lived long enough, he's now ready for the mastery stage. It is important to remember that the age of 42 was set with the assumption that martial arts instruction began at about age 5. Few of us today begin our training at that age.

I will be 42 next year, and I'm about as far from mastery as one can be while still being allowed in a dojo. Perhaps we should not set specific ages for specific ranks. But we ought to bear in mind the wisdom of earlier generations of martial artists. We ought to recognize, as they did, that certain components of our training simply can't be rushed. We need the patience to wait and anticipate the stages of training that are sure to follow if we pursue the way correctly. We should never expect a shortcut and always strive for maturity as a real *budoka*.

# ARE MARTIAL ARTS OATHS ANACHRONISTIC?

*November 1998*

"As I now undertake to receive training from you, I hereby swear that I will not display or teach even the most minor detail of your art to anyone, not even to members of my own family. Should I behave in a way contrary to this pledge, I resign myself to the punishment of the gods, great and small, of all Japan, especially the great deity Hachiman."
—*Oath of admission to the shibukawa ryu of jujutsu, circa 1700*

In a previous column, I examined the oaths that were once required before a student was admitted to most of the classical martial arts—the *koryu*—of old Japan. I traced this ritual back to the *kishomon,* the pledge that was sometimes taken by a samurai to demonstrate his loyalty to his lord. This practice began in the 13th century. The origins of the kishomon, in turn, can be found in the ninth century, the Heian era, in a custom called *genzan.* Genzan was the formal act of presenting oneself to a superior, or making an appearance.

By the time the warrior generals of the Kamakura era ruled Japan 400 years later, genzan had acquired a slightly different meaning. It described the process of a samurai going before the *shogun* and pledging allegiance to him. Those who were accepted were referred to as *go-kenin.* Later, they would be known as *hatamoto.* (If you've read *Shogun* or seen the movie, you might remember the scene in which John Blackthorne demands respect by shouting that he has been made a hatamoto by his patron, Lord Torinaga. At that stage of the action, however, Lord Torinaga was not a shogun and therefore would not have had the right to declare any of his vassals a hatamoto. He could, however, have promoted a man to the class of samurai.)

Later in the feudal period, the ritual of genzan became more formalized. The pledge was often followed by a mutual sharing of *sake,* and the lord would often present a gift in recognition of the event: a horse, weapon or helmet. Exactly when the kishomon became a part of this ritual is unclear. The term itself has Buddhist roots: It signified an oath sworn by the clergy of a temple. In this context, a kishomon was a promise to abide by the rules of the faith, but it also could include warnings of vengeance by deities if the pledge was broken.

By the 1400s, when the first historically verifiable koryu were being organized, the genzan/kishomon rituals had become a part of the life of the warrior. It was natural that a variation of them would be an integral part of joining and learning the methods of a school of combat.

As with the kishomon signed by the Buddhist priests, the oaths sworn by the martial arts exponent were usually explicit in what was expected of the swearer. He was forbidden to teach without permission or to divulge the secrets of the school. In some cases, he was obligated not to even use the methods of the school in open combat until given permission. In the oath taken by members of the *katori shinto ryu*, there is even a prohibition against "gambling of any sort" and visiting "disreputable places."

Equally explicit in these oaths were the punishments that could be expected should the pledge not be honored. In nearly every case, this punishment took a divine form. It usually came from the patron deity of the particular school, or from any of the Shinto or Buddhist gods that had special meaning to the warrior class. The deity Hachiman was often invoked. Hachiman was the deified spirit of Ojin, a second-century emperor and the ancestral leader of the Minamoto clan. In some schools, like the *katori ryu* and *shinkage ryu*, retribution could be expected from Marishiten-son, a goddess who was thought to reside near the North Star and to have ancient connections to the Japanese martial arts.

As I explained earlier, it's difficult for many of us in the present age to comprehend the seriousness with which these oaths were taken. But their content and meaning were the very heart of the classical martial arts school. The supernatural forces represented in deities like Marishiten-son and Hachiman were accepted tenets of any samurai's belief system. He sought their assistance and protection during needy times. He made an effort to conduct himself in a way that would curry their divine favor, and he certainly feared the retribution they might bring, should he disgrace the school to which he belonged.

As a relatively educated man of this century (and as a Christian, as well), my own experience in the classical martial arts of Japan has imbued me with a respect for these entities and the forces they represent. When I see traditional Japanese koryu misrepresented in videotaped demonstrations or in seminars open to any and all, my first reaction is to shudder for those who hold these oaths in such contempt. There can be a heavy price to pay for trespassing on these grounds.

The modern *budoka* is apt to dismiss all of this as superstition. For many who learn their arts in carpeted gyms with spas and juice bars, talk of loyalty and the intercession of supernatural beings sounds as quaint and primitive as a discussion of alchemy. It is my hope, however, that there are serious practitioners of karate and the other martial ways out there who will give some consideration to the oaths taken to uphold a tradition.

I would not encourage a karate *dojo* to include an oath as part of the process of training, and I don't want to hear about a bunch of samurai wannabes jabbing their fingers and writing their names in blood to prove their commitment. If you are not part of a tradition in which oaths are recognized, you can't create your own just by aping the form.

Instead, you must look behind the ritual itself and think about what it used to mean. The samurai joining a classical koryu understood that he was in the process of forging a link in a chain that stretched into the past—a chain of tradition which would, if he forged his link strong enough, also reach into the future. His loyalty to his school and his art represented a kind of selflessness. In becoming an expert in its methods, he improved the life of the school. There is in this attitude a sense of obligation that is always at the root of loyalty.

Now might be the time to ask yourself: What do I owe my art? How loyal am I?

# LOSING GRACEFULLY

*December 1998*

K onishiki retired earlier this year. He was one of the best *sumotori* of his generation and among the very best of the non-Japanese practitioners of the ancient art of *sumo*. The retirement of a great wrestler is always a sad affair, though it is rarely as pathetic as when most boxers finally throw in the towel. Unlike boxers—who might continue fighting long past the time when they should have stopped, taking on opponents far inferior or fighting with the risk of doing serious damage to themselves—sumotori generally go out when they are on top of their game or close to it. They do this because their trainers and fans encourage them to retire as soon as they start to falter and risk becoming an embarrassment to the art.

This illustrates the different perspectives in the Western sport of boxing and the Eastern art of sumo. The Western champion rarely thinks of what he owes his sport. His mentality is geared toward what he can get out of it. The sumotori, in contrast, is imbued with the traditions and standards of sumo from the first day of his training. He is more likely to retire to avoid damaging the reputation of his art, and fans and officials within the sumo community will applaud his decision.

Konishiki's retirement was particularly poignant because not long ago he was under serious consideration for promotion to the exalted level of *yokozuna*. The rank denotes far more than just a champion. It is a rare honor given to those sumotori who have earned not only a long and sterling string of victories, but who have also demonstrated character that is above reproach. Yokozuna are expected to embody everything noble about the art. It is taken so seriously that new yokozuna appear at a Shinto temple in Japan and ceremoniously announce themselves to the gods. The event is front-page news all over the country.

For a while, there was speculation that Konishiki would be promoted to yokozuna rank. There are many possible reasons why he was not—including racism, since Konishiki is not Japanese—but the Yokozuna Deliberation Council made an illuminating comment on the proposed promotion. A leader of the council said, "We didn't think his record was good enough. The way he lost was another consideration. He didn't look good when he was losing."

Read those last two lines again. They cut to the very essence of combative arts in which competition plays a role. The sumo officials believed that Konishiki lacked *hinkaku*. The word has a broad range of meanings:

dignity, good manners and strength of character.

Of course, on the battlefield or in a fight for one's life, hinkaku is not a primary consideration. But a sumo bout or a karate or judo match is not a fight to the death. There are rules and limitations and a certain decorum. This decorum, this sense of hinkaku, is at least as important as winning or losing. It is easier to be gracious and graceful in winning (though we have all seen examples of winners who were clumsy and boorish in their victory). The challenge lies in maintaining the proper attitude in defeat. This does not mean just being a "good loser"—bowing and shaking hands with the winner and not pouting or stomping around in disgust. No, hinkaku is something else.

Hinkaku, as it applies to one's attitude expressed after a loss, refers to the control of one's body, spirit and awareness. In a judo match, it means not flailing about spastically in the air while being thrown, trying desperately to land on one's feet or to make the fall look less serious and therefore undeserving of a point for an opponent. It means falling gracefully and skillfully so that one is relaxed and in control of his body, ready to come up again and continue.

In karate tournaments, the opposite of hinkaku is often evident. Losers slump in exasperation and disappointment, abandoning their composure entirely. They may instantly lose focus on their opponent, looking to the referee to question his decision.

The *karateka* with hinkaku maintains his concentration and continues to be aware of his opponent until the final bow. He keeps his body relaxed but on-guard, before and during the match. This is hinkaku, the absence of which kept Konishiki from the ranks of the yokozuna. Its presence is an unmistakable sign of the expert martial artist.

# THE BAFFLING CONCEPT OF THE KIAI
*January 1999*

The *kiai* is best known as an explosive shout or vocalization made during combat. It is undoubtedly one of those concepts that are intimately connected with the fighting arts. You could ask nearly any first-grader in the country how a karate guy sounds, and most would emit some of those grunts, shrieks, shouts and hoots that are the staple of action movies and television shows.

Unfortunately, even most serious practitioners of karate and other *budo* have little to add to this popular understanding of the kiai. I have never been in a karate *dojo* where the kiai was properly implemented. I have seen some dojo in which the practitioners actually shouted, "Key-eye!" as they trained. This would be equivalent to audiences at a football match cheering for their team by yelling, "Cheer!" At one *taekwondo* training hall I visited, enthusiasts went through the basics, throwing sets of three kicks or punches while shouting, "Tae! Kwon! Do!"

I cannot speak for the Korean combative arts, but in the Japanese budo, this so-called kiai is virtually a parody of the real thing. The same can be said for those erstwhile experts whose kiai sounded like the squawking of a jungle bird with its tail feathers caught in a trash compactor. In budo, the kiai is a fundamental concept of combat, one with vast ramifications. It is a concept of training, strategy and attitude that has multiple facets in the realms of the mental, spiritual and physical.

Initially, it is important to understand that the word "kiai" has no precise definition within the fighting arts of Japan. Particularly in some classical schools *(koryu)*, the word is used to mean "volition" or "commitment." If my training partner is attacking me with enough determination to actually make his technique work, he forces me to meet it and deal with it correctly. He is demonstrating what many classical systems would call kiai. The use of the word in this way makes sense if one considers that it is composed of the Japanese characters for *ki* (energy) and *ai* (meeting or joining).

This definition of kiai can also refer to one's entire mental state when focused on an activity. That is what the great warlord Hideyoshi Toyotomi was referring to when he praised the kiai of Sen no Rikyu, the master who taught Hideyoshi the art of the tea ceremony. Hideyoshi was talking with one of his best and fiercest generals, Kato Kiyomasa. "Rikyu's kiai is so strong," Hideyoshi said, "that even though he has no training as a warrior, when he is preparing a bowl of tea, I cannot find a single moment where

he might be vulnerable to an attack."

Kato, being the sort who would have tested someone who said the sun sets in the West before he would believe it, decided to test Rikyu. Some time later, he and Hideyoshi were guests in Rikyu's tea hut. Rikyu was making tea, and Kato was watching him every second. It did indeed seem that there was no gap in Rikyu's mental concentration and poise. Then Kato thought he saw an opening. He held a fan, thinking that he could lift it and whack Rikyu over the head. Just as he thought this, however, Rikyu suddenly turned and looked directly at him. "You have a fine retainer in Kato Kiyomasa," he said to Hideyoshi, appearing to be simply making conversation. But the story goes that he locked onto Kato with a stare that caused Kato to lose his breath and completely destroyed his thoughts of attack. This is kiai in the classical sense of the word.

In modern budo like karate, though, kiai is used to refer to a focus of energy expressed through vocalization. This is far too narrow a definition. A true kiai can be completely without sound; this is an idea that more advanced *karateka* should consider carefully. Where sound is used in implementing a kiai, the modern exponent might be surprised to learn that not just any shout or noise will do. In the feudal-era koryu, each system had its own distinctive kiai. A person knowledgeable about these systems could easily distinguish the particular koryu just by listening to it. In some instances, these distinctive sounds had their origins in Buddhist theology. In others, they had evolved to be particularly effective in performing specific techniques.

# IMPROVE YOUR ABILITY TO "LISTEN"

*February 1999*

Try this for an exercise: Stand facing your training partner, both of you in a front stance with your left leg leading. Your opponent takes a full step in with his right leg and punches at your solar plexus with his right fist. When he does, shift a little to your left with your left leg still leading. At the same time, move a bit toward your partner. When you do, touch your open left hand to the outside of his elbow. From there, carefully execute a ridgehand strike to his temple.

Sounds simple. It isn't. I'd wager a hefty chunk of change that you can't do it correctly. Notice that I said to touch your left hand to his elbow, not block it or swat it away. Notice also that I said to keep your hand open. This is vital. What you are doing is making contact in such a way that you can detect the level of energy in your opponent's arm and the direction in which it is flowing without striking it or smothering it. In some Chinese combative arts, this is referred to as *ting jing*, or "listening energy."

Simply put, this is extremely advanced karate. Without at least 10 years of practice under an expert instructor, forget it. Your body simply won't have the suppleness or the ability to relax in the middle of the action, and your mind won't have the awareness to make this kind of technique work.

---

What you are doing is making contact in such a way that you can detect the level of energy in your opponent's arm and the direction in which it is flowing without striking it or smothering it.

---

*Karateka* with less experience should sharpen their blocking or evading skills. But they should remember, too, that these talents are not the ultimate in karate strategy, nor are they likely to be very effective against a fighter who knows what he's doing.

Try a block with your right inner forearm in which your fist travels in a counterclockwise motion against an opponent's straight punch, and you will destroy the balance of the puncher and lead his attack off harmlessly—unless he's good. If he's good, as soon as your block makes contact with his attacking arm, he'll relax and use your energy—with his elbow as a hinge—and you'll find a hand slapping you smartly between your legs. True, there won't be any strong hip action behind his strike—as too many karateka have been led to believe is absolutely necessary for a good strike. Nonetheless, you will be in a world of hurt.

At karate's advanced levels, there is no "blocking" in the sense that you commonly think of that word. Instead, you try to make contact with a strike in such a way that you can "hear" its power and energy and then deal with it. That's what this exercise is designed to teach. You move out of the way of the attack. It would be foolish to stand in its path and assume that you have the strength and timing to redirect or destroy it. But if all you do is avoid it, you will just have to deal with a follow-up strike. So while you use body positioning to escape, you're also using your hand to make contact and begin to control your opponent's energy so you can use it or find the weakness in it.

You will likely encounter some problems when you begin this exercise:

• You will make contact with the elbow of your opponent's attacking arm, but you will have turned to the side so far that the other side of your body will be useless to you. That's why you should practice the follow-up ridgehand strike. If it seems awkward, that's because you've rotated too far. Keep your body's center pointed directly at your opponent so your right hand is able to make a strong attack.

• You will touch the punching elbow, but your left arm will be tight against your chest. In this case, you have misjudged the focus of your partner's punch and he's "jammed" you. There's only one way to get over this, and that is to practice so you can determine—even while it's happening—how deeply he's entering with his attack. Then you can adjust your counter accordingly. The secret here is in your initial gaze and the movement of his hips.

• In contacting your opponent's elbow, you swat or push rather than touch. This is an important point to work on. You want the natural curve of your palm to fit over his elbow, giving you maximum contact to feel the movement. To do this, your wrist and arm must be relaxed—the hand not grabbing or pushing but "touching." How do you do it? You practice. A lot.

# ORIGINS OF THE OKINAWAN STAFF

*April 1999*

The *bo*, or long staff, is one of the most popular weapons in the Okinawan arts. Although it has a long history in the Ryukyu Islands, no one is sure about the details. Many martial arts historians believe that it evolved from the *tenbin*, a long stick that was balanced across a person's shoulders to carry buckets of water. It's a plausible theory. But to hold the cords for the buckets, the tenbin was notched at each end. Because the *kontei*, or tip of the staff, is its most important striking surface, the notched tenbin would have had limited use as a weapon; it was weak at the ends and would likely have snapped when striking a target. While it's nice to think of Okinawan farmers carrying buckets with their tenbin and ditching the water when they were attacked, the notched tenbin would not have done the job.

It's more likely that the bo was intended to be a weapon from the outset, not some other implement pressed into action in an emergency. But was it a weapon native to Okinawa, or were its methods imported from China or elsewhere?

The earliest written reference to the bo comes from a text on 14th-century Okinawan culture, which mentions only that Okinawans used staffs for fighting. But by that time, the Chinese had been trading in Okinawa,

> There is such a wide variety of staff techniques from mainland China and so many different ways of employing the weapon that it would be impossible to determine the "Chinese way" of using the staff.

and certainly some Chinese culture had been transmitted. For instance, the word "bo" is of Japanese origin, but an older Ryukyu term for the weapon is *kon* or *kun*. This term probably came from the Fukien dialect of mainland China, where the staff was called a *kuang*. Even today, the Okinawan bo *kata* are known as *shushi no kon* or *arakaki no kon*.

It is more difficult to trace the origins of the kata themselves. There is such a wide variety of staff techniques from mainland China and so many different ways of employing the weapon that it would be impossible to determine the "Chinese way" of using the staff. Still, we see certain movements and methods in many of the older Okinawan bo kata that seem to indicate a Chinese influence.

For instance, in most kata, the bo is not struck against the imaginary target in a flat, angular way. Instead, it is usually given a little twist with the wrist at the moment of contact. That explains a saying often heard in the Okinawan *dojo*: The strength of the bo lies in the wrists. Real bo technique demands great wrist strength and flexibility. The wrists "snap" the bo as it strikes. The proper hitting action with the bo is never angular; it is always oblique and circular. This is often seen in the Chinese arts.

On the other hand, some researchers have noted that most Okinawan bo methods call for it to be held with both hands, each placed about one-third of the way from the end. Although there are notable exceptions, most Chinese staff forms feature techniques in which the weapon is held at one end and its full length is either swung or thrust. Even in the Japanese classical martial traditions, both hands are placed on one end, allowing for a longer striking implement that keeps the enemy farther away. The evenly spaced grip used in Okinawa appears to be unique. If the Okinawans were so strongly influenced by the Chinese, why do their bo basics bear no resemblance to Chinese methods?

There will never be definitive answers to these questions. Written records and oral histories are either absent or so layered with legend that they're rendered useless. Most of the kata for the bo, as well as for other Okinawan weapons, cannot be reliably dated to any time before the mid-18th century, when kata were first catalogued. Before that, most of the methods of bo training were not kata in the proper sense; rather, they were informal collections of techniques passed from teacher to student.

I suspect that the Chinese staff arts did influence the Okinawan arts because Okinawa experienced such a strong influx of Chinese methods in other combative arts—and in its culture in general. The Okinawans were not stupid. If they saw the Chinese staff in action and deemed it effective, they would have incorporated those techniques into their own. However, the Okinawans did have bo techniques and methods that were purely of their own making.

I also suspect that there were two different approaches to fighting with the bo: methods used by the upper classes (police, royalty, etc.) and methods used by everyone else (farmers, fishermen, etc.). The upper classes would have had more exposure to Chinese teachings. Their bo kata and techniques would have reflected this influence more than those of the lower classes. If this theory is correct, we might be able to classify a bo kata not only by its creator or point of geographical origin but also by whether its chief inspiration was Okinawan or Chinese.

# ULTIMATE FIGHTING IN JAPAN—100 YEARS AGO!

*June 1999*

A frequent characteristic of the thoroughly modern person—the kind who believes he's on the cutting edge—is ignorance of a simple fact: Whatever he's invented or created or postulated has almost certainly been done before. In fact, chances are it was done better previously, as well.

A good example of this comes in the form of those who believe that pitting combatants of various fighting arts against one another is a late 20th-century invention. One hundred years ago, the Japanese were doing much the same thing.

When feudalism was abolished in 1867, the lives of thousands of samurai were turned upside down. Having been part of a caste system that classified their families as warriors for, in some instances, nearly 1,000 years, these men suddenly found themselves without any of the structure or philoso-

---

**These were a series of contests often lasting for more than a week and pitting martial artists against one another to entertain crowds that paid to watch.**

---

phy that had constituted their way of life. More practically, they were also without jobs. In the West, aspects of this part of Japanese history have remained nearly secret. It was a very harsh era, particularly for the former samurai. Times were so difficult for many of them that they were forced to sell everything they owned just to buy food. Some starved to death. It was a desperate moment for a group that had virtually every aspect of its existence yanked away.

One solution for the former samurai came with the creation of *gekiken kogyo*. These were a series of contests often lasting for more than a week and pitting martial artists against one another to entertain crowds that paid to watch. Rules were laid out, standard sizes and lengths for mock weapons were established, and entrance fees and prizes were set.

The creation of gekiken kogyo was claimed to be instructional. A central figure behind it was Sakakibara Kenkichi, a prominent figure in the history of early *kendo* and an expert swordsman who, like many others of his kind, had been reduced to unemployment and destitution. Supposedly, Sakakibara reasoned that, if the masses (who had never seen martial arts intended solely for the warrior) could watch the "real thing," they'd have an appreciation for the value of those disciplines.

That may indeed have been the motivation, but reality was something else. Not long after the first gekiken kogyo in 1873, carnival-type barkers

were hawking dramatic matches between exponents of different schools. Popular matchups included women fighting men, contestants of vastly different sizes and experts with unusual weapons. The competitions took on the aura of a sideshow, with all kinds of glitz and spectacle. The contests were held in amphitheaters and other venues around the country. Posters announced the big names competing. Attendance numbered into the thousands, with everyone cheering on the gladiators and screaming for their champion. Does this sound similar to any modern-day event?

Predictably, a concerned government got involved. Within a few months of the peak of popularity of these shows, they were banned by official decree. It was not just the government that opposed the gekiken kogyo; senior martial arts exponents from every part of Japan denounced them in newspapers and magazines, describing them as nothing more than money-making schemes devoid of a sense of wisdom and shame.

Sakakibara soon realized that, despite whatever noble hopes he'd had for the presentations, they were just as awful as their detractors claimed. He was disappointed that the contests' rules and tactics created new strategies that had little relevance to real combat, and he was saddened by the emphasis on showmanship, vanity and greed that separated the contests from the way of the warrior. A trio of wealthy friends set him up with a *dojo* that shared space with a *sake* shop, but Sakakibara was never comfortable trying to teach the martial ways in such an environment, and that enterprise soon failed, as well. Sakakibara died in 1894, still regretting his involvement in the fighting contests.

While explaining his city's ban on the contests, the mayor of Kyoto expressed some sentiments that are worth pondering today: "These gekiken kogyo aren't much more than peddling the names of those participating. Even worse, they deceive people and expose them to violence. [The participants] would be much better off using their energies for real work, striving to have a healthy and meaningful life."

# THE SPIRIT OF THE WEAPON
*July 1999*

When I was training with my Okinawan karate teachers, both were attending graduate school with scholarships from the U.S. government. They were well-educated men who were very modern in their outlook, well-traveled and cosmopolitan. But in some ways, they were very traditional, and I was often reminded of that.

After I had trained for a few years, my teachers introduced me to the weapons of Okinawan combat. Among them was the *sai*. I was working on a form called *aragaki*, which requires a pair of the instruments. The two that my teachers had given me had their handles wrapped in cloth to make them easier to grip, and they had been made the traditional way—with molten iron poured into a mold. I was expected to treat them with respect.

In modern *dojo*, even in Okinawa, sai are often mounted on pegs on the wall. In the old days, however, there were no dojo; training was conducted outside. A *karateka's* sai, as well as his other weapons, were kept at home, and they were usually hidden. My *sensei* kept this pair on a shelf in his kitchen so they would be handy in case someone tried to break in. But, as is the case with many things Okinawan, I soon discovered that things often have more than one explanation.

After practicing the aragaki *kata* in the backyard, I walked into the house and headed for the shower. Instead of returning the sai to the kitchen, I put them on the counter. By the time I finished showering, I had forgotten about them. The next morning, one of my sensei began questioning my commitment to my training: How could I expect to learn karate when I couldn't even remember a simple thing like putting things back where they belonged? I apologized without making excuses—and made certain never to do that again. That night, the sensei introduced me to the concept of *shiyaru*.

In Japanese, *aru* means "to exist" or "to have." *Shi* is a more complex word from the Ryukyu dialect that refers to the quality or "personality" of an inanimate object. Do you have a favorite screwdriver or pen? Is there a golf club or baseball glove you've used for so long that it seems to have its own personality? When we spend a lot of time with an object, we tend to personalize it, imbue it with a specialness that distinguishes it from others. Hand a *kendo* practitioner a *shinai* that's not his regular training weapon, and he will not even need to look at it to know it doesn't belong to him. Bamboo practice swords may all look alike to outsiders, but to the

87

kendo practitioner, his shinai has a unique feel to it. The Okinawans call that shiyaru.

Like all technologically simple people, the Okinawans relied on fishing and farming to make a living, and the tools they used were meant to last. The fisherman used an oar, which after years of use became personalized—just as did the farmer's sickle. So it was natural that the Okinawan karateka's weapons would be afforded the same considerations. We're not talking just of "customizing" a weapon to make it work better for the user. Shiyaru refers to a spiritual or magical quality. The sai in my teacher's home had shiyaru. To keep it, the pair needed to be cared for and kept in the proper place.

Weapons used by Okinawan karateka were kept in special places, my sensei explained, because if an enemy found them, he could disrupt the shiyaru they had. In a sense, an enemy could cause them to lose some of their personality and potency. I read a Western karateka's recollection of his training in Okinawa, in which he described buying a new *bo* and showing it to his sensei. The teacher advised him to strip off the lacquer finish so that, during practice, the oils from his hands would penetrate the weapon and protect it better. That would also develop the weapon's shiyaru, the sensei claimed.

I have long suspected a link exists between the cultures of Okinawa and other regions of southeast Asia. Shiyaru may be a clue to this link. Consider the *kris*, the bladed weapon of Indonesia. There are numerous stories about the ability of a good kris to vibrate in its scabbard to warn the wearer of approaching danger. This folk belief is consistent with the Okinawan attitude regarding shiyaru and might indicate a connection between Okinawa and other parts of Asia.

I don't know whether shiyaru exists. I do know that the heavy gardening *kama* (sickles) I use for weeding and other tasks have a balance that, after years of use, works perfectly for my arm length and strength. I know that a pair of *hera* (hoes) I had was fine until I separated the two implements accidentally one autumn, leaving one in the garden shed and the other in my shop. Both rusted.

Whether or not shiyaru is real, my sai will stay hidden together.

# DRESSING THE PART

*August 1999*

The *keikogi* is a familiar part of most modern *dojo*. Westerners like to call it a *gi*, the truncated form of the word, but to Japanese ears, the term is a rather crude abbreviation.

Just as crude is the metamorphosis the keikogi has undergone in the West. Starting in the 1970s, it was subjected to all sorts of customizing. Colors other than the traditional white began appearing, and *karateka* started sewing goofy patches on the sleeves and legs. Then came bell-bottom trousers and the inevitable displays of ego and advertising with names and school logos emblazoned across the back. Even with all these modifications, most martial artists assumed the keikogi was as essential to karate as punching and kicking.

Time marches on, though, and the question of whether martial artists need to wear a uniform is being raised more and more. The reason for the question may be mercantile in origin. Proprietors of many karate schools note that one thing that keeps potential students from enrolling is that they think they will look silly in a baggy, pajama-like keikogi.

---

**People who gracefully accept discomfort and the possibility of looking awkward and "uncool" are exactly the sort of people that are welcome in a real *dojo*.**

---

They're absolutely right about this. The beginning karateka, standing about self-consciously in a uniform still starchy-stiff and creased, his belt incorrectly knotted and askew, does not cut a terribly suave figure. So why not take a cue from the fitness studios and allow leotards, sweat pants, tank tops and T-shirts? Why not allow whatever people would feel comfortable wearing while working out at home or mowing the lawn?

For the vast majority of the establishments that pass for karate schools in this country, that argument has a great deal of merit. Those places are nothing more than specialized fitness gyms. There is no sense of the spiritual component of karate. There is no sense of belonging to a tradition, of following as closely as possible a path that was laid out by previous generations. Narcissism permeates the landscape. The desire to look good is nearly as important as the desire to feel good, and both those needs far outweigh any desire to polish one's spirit to accomplish good. That is fine for those who want it, and spandex is perfectly appropriate in such a setting. It has no place, however, on the floor of a real karate dojo.

The person interested in seriously pursuing karate begins by recognizing that what he is about to enter is different from normal activities. If it were not, why would he bother? Why take up something like karate if more familiar, more economical and more accessible pastimes like softball or aerobics will suffice for physical fitness or socializing?

The person about to seriously take up karate knows there is something about the art that he wants in his life. He may not be sure how it is different—almost certainly the beginner does not know this—but he knows it's there and wants to be part of it.

The wearing of a keikogi is a physical way of establishing that this activity is not like any other. It's true that beginners look awkward in a new keikogi. Despite what you may think, they'd look nearly the same no matter what they wore because, when people try the basic movements of an unfamiliar art, they always appear awkward. Part of any serious *budo* training is coming face to face with this awkwardness, acknowledging it and attempting to overcome it.

Being willing to put on a strange uniform is actually one of the least uncomfortable challenges faced by new karateka. They must also contend with an odd and new terminology. Even native speakers of Japanese must deal with this, for the vocabulary of the dojo includes dozens of words not used in everyday life. Also, they must deal with modes of behavior quite different from those they encounter during their normal activities.

One can probably teach karate in a way that avoids these discomforts, but to do so is to wander off the path of the budo—make no mistake about it.

People who gracefully accept discomfort and the possibility of looking awkward and "uncool" are exactly the sort of people that are welcome in a real dojo. There aren't a lot of these folks around—not as many, to be sure, as are attracted to exercise gyms. And that's fine, because a dojo and a gym—no matter what anyone says—are entirely different places.

# TWO WAYS OF "NOT THINKING"

September 1999

We often hear of geniuses—writers, scientists, composers, etc.—who become enthralled with the project on which they are working. They go at it for days, forgetting about their need to bathe or sleep or even eat. Totally absorbed in their task, they are oblivious to the world around them. In the Japanese *budo*, this state of mind is called *muga muchu*. Muga means "no thought" or "a mind unconscious of itself." Muchu means "stupor" or "hypnotic state."

Imagine a *karateka* standing in front of the *makiwara*, punching and punching. He is immersed in the action of driving his fist against the pad again and again. Time disappears. Outside distractions disappear. He does not know whether he has punched 100 times or 1,000 times. There could be a five-car pileup on the street in front of the *dojo*, and he would not be aware of it because he is so focused. That is muga muchu.

An athlete might view muga muchu as a goal—a "runner's high" mentality that allows him to ignore distractions and reach a state of maximum performance. A martial artist, on the other hand, would probably view muga muchu as a luxury he can seldom afford. He strives, instead, for

---

**The *karateka* must deal with a number of complex factors in his training, including distance, timing and rhythm.**

---

*muga no kyochi.* Kyochi means "state" or "condition"—in this case, a mental state.

Imagine the same makiwara with a different karateka in front of it. This one is also punching and punching, but he's aware of what's going on around him. He's cognizant of his junior in the dojo standing off to the side, possibly wanting a turn at the post himself or some instruction in the proper way to hit it. The karateka is also aware that the teacher's daughter is having a birthday celebration tonight and that the teacher might want to close the dojo a little early. He knows that the thwack-thwack-thwack of his punching might eventually bother the occupants of the office next door, especially on a warm night when all the windows are open. This karateka is in a state of muga no kyochi.

To understand the difference between a runner and a martial artist, you must remember that the runner is usually on a clearly marked course with safety provisions made by the race committee. The karateka must deal with a number of complex factors in his training, including distance, timing and rhythm. These change on a second-by-second basis. He must also deal with uneven surfaces or weather conditions that can affect his performance. That is one reason why it's critical to train outside with some regularity. Muga muchu might be fine in some isolated circumstances, but for the most part, concentrating while continuing to maintain an awareness of all that is going on around you is what you should aim for.

How do you avoid being distracted if you are not totally focused? The answer is that awareness of a phenomenon is not the same as responding to that phenomenon. I remember once demonstrating *iaido*, the art of drawing and cutting with the Japanese sword, at an indoor event. Just as I began, a hideous shriek sounded. It was a fire alarm. I'd like to say it was my sense of muga no kyochi that enabled me to meet this challenge. Truth is, it was simply a sense of not knowing what else to do but carry on. I heard someone mutter that the alarm had been malfunctioning all week, and I could see that no one in the crowd was rushing for the door. So I continued.

Would I have done so if everyone had stood up to leave or if I had smelled smoke? Perhaps if I had been in muga muchu. That might have been impressive—continuing to draw and cut while the building burned around me, remaining totally absorbed in my art. But it wouldn't have been very smart.

Instead of attributing my continuation of the iaido demonstration to muga muchu, I attribute it to having considered the factors of the situation and having found no reason not to go on.

Afterward, a couple of people complimented me on my calmness in the face of the distraction. Was I even aware of the alarm, they asked? Of course I was aware of it—and of the comments about it and the reaction of the crowd. I was not in a state of muga no kyochi, but I was on the right track.

# THREE TIPS FOR BETTER LEARNING
*December 1999*

"It took me almost 10 years in the *dojo* to learn how to learn," a martial artist once said. This is an interesting comment. Most people come to the martial arts with at least some schooling behind them. They assume that they know how to learn and that the real task is mastering the material before them—the techniques and the *kata*. They don't often consider that the actual ways in which they assimilate what is presented will have an impact on their progress. How they learn in the dojo is at least as important as what they learn. For this reason, I will present three strategies for improving how you learn.

First, learn to be flexible in your perspective. In his book on martial strategy, the legendary swordsman Miyamoto Musashi warned that in battle you can become too focused on minor details. You risk becoming too involved in a small part of the conflict without seeing the overall situation. Learn to pull back mentally, he advised. Look at the bigger picture.

That advice directly applies to learning techniques. When a teacher demonstrates an intricate movement—a joint lock, for instance—students may fixate on the minute manipulations of the hands or fingers. They assume that is the crux of the technique and direct all their attention there. When they adopt this method of learning, they miss the broader action. The teacher's body shifting may be what makes the technique work. Get that

---

**Be willing to sublimate your ego and your desire to have your teacher believe you are competent.**

---

shift down, and you will have learned the fundamentals for that technique and probably others. In general, when you are introduced to new material in the dojo, focus your attention on the broader aspects rather than on the finer details that can be polished later.

You will often see a skilled teacher appear to gaze off absentmindedly when he's supposed to be observing class. True, he might simply be bored. If he's good, though, it's more likely that he's deliberately focusing his look past the student. Try it. You will miss some of the particulars of what you're looking at, but you will see some aspects that you might not notice otherwise.

Remember, too, that the opposite can be true. Watching the action unfold on the whole battlefield gives you a general picture, but you have to be careful of that fellow slipping up behind you to cut you in half. Find a balance. Avoid concentrating too much on either way.

Second, be willing to appear stupid. Be willing to sublimate your ego and your desire to have your teacher believe you are competent. Often, a student will be stuck at one spot in a kata. He knows the entire sequence but can't get past that spot. The teacher comes and demonstrates. As soon as the teacher gets to the student's sticking point, the student says, "Now I remember!" More often than not, the student will make it past that point, only to get stuck again a few movements later.

If a teacher begins to demonstrate anything for you, don't do or say anything that will stop him. Watch everything he offers, even if you're convinced you know it better than he does. If you don't, you're apt to be embarrassed a second time when you still can't remember the technique. And more important, you will have missed an opportunity to see a senior perform.

In a similar situation, you are practicing and your teacher tells you to freeze. It's natural to want to let him know that you know what you're doing wrong, so when he tells you to stop, you are tempted to correct your mistake. Often, your self-correction is not a correction at all. The teacher must then ask you to go through the movement again until you get to where your original mistake occurred. If a teacher commands you to stop, do it.

Third, be open to new learning experiences. I once saw a student being taught a new kata with a staff. The sequence of movements was very similar to those of another kata, but there was a significant difference that involved a change in the grip. The student assumed it was exactly the same as what he already knew. The teacher kept going over the sequence, smiling and shaking his head as the student made the same mistake. It was an illuminating lesson for observers.

Of course, an essential part of learning is building on what you already know. You will never progress at all if you can't rely on what you have learned in the past. But you must avoid becoming too reliant on what you know. Examples of this pitfall frequently occur at seminars in which an unfamiliar art is taught. For instance, students with an extensive karate background who try to learn *tai chi chuan* are often able to see the new art only through the filter of their karate experience. They wind up with a weird hybrid because they have not learned how to learn. Try to avoid falling into the same trap.

# THE GUYS UNDER THE FLOOR

*January 2000*

The Japanese have an interesting expression: *en no shita no chikaramo-chi.* It refers to the *chikara* (power) of a room's architecture being below it. It's often used to refer to a person who, like the pillars and foundation that support the house, is unseen or "under the floor" of a company, group or organization, propping it up and keeping it sound.

If you want to know the difference between a successful *dojo* and an unsuccessful one, you should look underneath and see who's there. Often, we tend to overlook this. The teacher and senior students who donate their time to teach classes are obviously important to the dojo's success. It's clear, too, that patrons provide the funds needed to keep the dojo going. Not so obvious are those individuals who make their contributions quietly or unobtrusively.

Under-the-floor people are not unique to the *budo* dojo. Churches, civic groups and other organizations also have them. In fact, they're almost essential. But if you think about it, you'll realize that there are more of them in your dojo than you previously realized: the student who fixed the shower drain when it kept backing up, the one who repaired the fan, and the one who took charge when the new floor was installed. They are a particular kind of under-the-floor people who handle the *zatsumu*, the miscellaneous

---

**Not so obvious are those individuals who make their contributions [to the *dojo*] quietly or unobtrusively.**

---

jobs that crop up. Called *shuzen-sha* or *nandemoyaru-nin*, they are handymen who can take care of any situation. Without them, it would cost a fortune to hire professional plumbers, electricians and the like.

If your dojo is big enough, you probably have someone who has taken on the responsibility of being the receptionist/greeter—most likely a senior student. At the end of class, he or she will look at the people who've come to watch. Most of them will be parents or friends, but if there's a stranger, the senior will be able to ascertain whether the visitor is interested in joining the class. It's an interpersonal skill I certainly don't have, but I've seen it used time after time. The senior approaches the stranger and explains how the dojo works, what's going on and what's required for joining.

We tend to hear too much about *shihan* (masters) or *shidoin* (instruc-

THE BEST OF DAVE LOWRY

tors) and not nearly enough about the under-the-floor people. When the dojo is preparing to travel to a tournament or seminar or when it's time to plan a picnic or party, you'll notice that the responsibilities for all the logistics tend to fall on these people. They make sure there are enough drivers, that meals are arranged, and that all participants know when and where they're supposed to be. The students responsible for that may not be senior members of the dojo, but they are the true *shihainin* (managers) of the school.

There may be a board of directors at your dojo, called the *riji-kai*. The members are likely to make financial and other decisions about the school. This board is probably made up of senior members of the dojo who have advanced experience in the art. In some cases, there may be associate or honorary members of the riji-kai who are not so advanced but whose nonmartial arts skills are invaluable. If, for example, you have a certified public accountant who begins training at the dojo, he may be asked to be a financial consultant. A lawyer may serve as a legal adviser. While they may not have a high standing in the dojo hierarchy, their assistance is essential to its successful operation.

# AN AIKIDO TECHNIQUE FOR KARATE STUDENTS
*April 2000*

A *sensei* named Matsui, who had trained in the classical martial traditions and faced numerous enemies in combat, rarely had good things to say about any of the modern martial arts. He tended to dismiss them all as noncombative and more appropriate for sport than for real life. He had criticized *aikido* in particular. So I was surprised one day to hear him say something good about aikido. He said its principle of *tenkai* (body rotation) was effective and essential for learning to deal with serious attacks. That caused me to do a lot of thinking about tenkai, and I continue to explore it to this day.

If you don't know what tenkai is, assume the relaxed, mostly upright stance you use while sparring. Your feet will probably be about 45 degrees off centerline, and if you're right-handed, your left leg will be in front. Now, pivot 180 degrees on the balls of your feet. If you were initially facing the front of the *dojo*, you're now looking at the rear, and your right leg is leading. This is tenkai. It seems easy, but it's actually difficult to pivot smoothly and quickly while keeping your balance.

To see the possible applications of tenkai, have a partner simulate a straight knife thrust to your chest. The average *karateka* will be tempted

---

Because it changes your spatial relationship with your opponent in ways you've probably never encountered, experimenting with *tenkai* can create many new opportunities and ideas.

---

to perform an inner block, deflecting the line of the attack and using the rotation of his hips to add power and snap. That's fine. But assume now that you're on a crowded subway or walking down Bourbon Street during Mardi Gras, where space is tight, or perhaps your arms are encumbered because you're carrying two heavy bags. There are situations in which your body mass has to rotate away from the line of attack. In essence, this is tenkai—when you "block" without blocking. Your hip deployment will be very similar to the rotation you use to make a regular block, but you must continue it until you face the opposite direction.

A second, more important reason to perfect tenkai becomes obvious when you face multiple assailants. Most forms of karate are not designed for encounters with more than a single enemy. Sporting competition has placed an inordinate emphasis on one-on-one battles. Even without competition to blame, karate has always concentrated much of its strategy on the single attacker.

Often, karateka assume that *kata* contain methods for fighting multiple opponents. Instead of taking this for granted, the advanced practitioner should make a detailed study of how the techniques in kata flow from one opponent to the other. There is one kata, usually practiced by upper-level karateka, that contains a tenkai-like move. Do you know it? (Hint: It involves shifting back and forth while throwing a pair of downward punches.)

Even if you're convinced that your karate has sufficient shifting techniques, there is still considerable benefit in learning tenkai. Begin your study as I explained earlier—in a relaxed, mostly upright position. On the balls of your feet, shift so you're facing what was behind you. Go slowly. If you move too quickly, you'll over-rotate. If you use your shoulders to begin the motion, you won't have control when you finish. When you can turn while retaining your balance, have a partner stand in front of you and slowly front kick your midsection. Because you're working on timing, he should not use a lot of power. Do a tenkai to avoid the kick, letting it go past as you turn.

When you can rotate and let the kick pass, a little bulb ought to go off over your head: "What if I slide in a bit as the kick starts, *then* do a tenkai?" Try it and look where you are when the kick fully extends—right where you need to be for a mild push to topple your opponent. Your choice of counters is extensive.

Because it changes your spatial relationship with your opponent in ways you've probably never encountered, experimenting with tenkai can create many new opportunities and ideas. No matter which style of karate you study, tenkai is definitely worth investigating.

# THE MYSTERIOUS CASE OF THE KOREAN NUNCHAKU

*May 2000*

A Korean *nunchaku?* I had to admit it: I was stumped. Of course I hadn't seen every Asian weapon, but a Korean nunchaku? I'd never heard of such a thing until I saw it in a martial arts magazine—not *Black Belt*, but one of those publications that never recovered after ninjas faded in popularity. Nonetheless, the article about the Korean nunchaku appeared to be a serious one, so I took it that way.

According to the author, the Koreans developed something incredibly similar to the agricultural tool that Okinawans called the nunchaku—supposedly without any Ryukyuan influences. Like the Okinawans, the Koreans had originally used the instrument for threshing rice and later adapted it as a weapon. The article mentioned that the two pieces of the Korean nunchaku were cylindrical and had a short chain connecting them, while the Okinawan version had a horsehair cord. Several photos demonstrated

---

## If we investigate claims regarding the existence of a Korean *nunchaku*, who knows what more profound questions might be answered?

---

the weapon's combative applications; most of the sequences resembled the antics of actors who use the nunchaku in cinematic battles.

Although the article was fascinating, it was a bit of a mystery. I'd never heard of Koreans using this weapon. None of the texts I have on Korean arts mentioned it. None of the practitioners of Korean arts I know had heard of it.

My first step was to visit the Asian library of a nearby university. There, in a book titled *Koreans and Their Culture*, I found a lengthy description of Korean rice agriculture in pre-modern times. A rope was wrapped around sheaves of dried rice still on the stalk. Then, the sheaves were banged on a hard wooden mortar to separate the grain from the chaff. A nunchaku-type thresher was not mentioned.

My next step was to ask a friend whose mother and grandmother were born and raised in rural Korea. They remembered when they first got an automatic, gas-powered thresher. Before that, they said, they used the rope-knotting method. I described the nunchaku, but they said they had never heard of such a thing being used on a Korean farm. I asked about the Korean term that the author had used for the weapon. They said it was just a couple words that mean "stick and chain."

I contacted the Korean Embassy. Yes, they said, way back in the old days before machinery did the work, rice in Korea was threshed by tying a rope around a bundle, then shaking or flinging it to separate the grains. No, they had never heard of the implement I described.

Now I was really curious. How could Korean martial artists have developed the thresher into a weapon if it had never been used as a thresher in the first place? I had reached a dead end. I couldn't think of any more steps to take, short of tracking down the author of the article. Then I might ask a few questions about topics he neglected to cover: What evidence do you have that the nunchaku was used in Korea? Are there any examples in museums there? Are there any descriptions in Korean literature? Who taught the instructor you interviewed how to use the weapon? Did he get the techniques he demonstrated from a Korean farmer?

If we investigate claims regarding the existence of a Korean nunchaku, who knows what more profound questions might be answered? On the other hand, some mysteries are better left unsolved.

# JAPAN'S KOREAN CONNECTION
*July 2000*

One of the criticisms Japanese *karateka* often level at Korean *taekwondo* is that it lacks aesthetic integrity—it is commercially driven and its forms are perfunctory nods at "art." Most important, they claim that taekwondo and other Korean disciplines have made efforts to cover up or deny their obvious Japanese roots. I believe there is ample evidence that these criticisms are largely on target. However, karateka should not be too smug about this. Rather, they ought to acknowledge what modern Japanese karate owes to Korean culture.

Soetsu Yanagi (1889-1961) was a pivotal figure in the history of Japanese art. He founded the *minshukuteki kogei (mingei* for short, which means "folk art") movement, which galvanized the art world of Japan during the first decades of the 20th century. Yanagi stressed the value of simple folk art, the ordinary beauty found in objects used in everyday life, and he discovered this beauty in—of all places—Korea.

In 1916, Yanagi, who was obsessed with the ceramics of Korea's Yi dynasty, visited the neighboring country. The pots, jugs and bowls he found were not the fine, elegant porcelain of the upper classes. They were made by rural craftsmen and had a rough, often uneven texture and shape. They were not fancy because they were made to be used, not admired. Their beauty came as a natural result of their function.

This was not the first time in Japanese history that Korean art had a far-reaching effect on Japanese aesthetics. Centuries before, the tea master Sen no Rikyu turned his back on the elaborate grandeur of the aristocratic approach to the tea ceremony and created a ceremony with simple, rustic implements. Rikyu used the rice bowls of Korean farmers as tea bowls, and they serve as the model for tea ceremony bowls today.

Yanagi's folk art movement had a tremendous effect on Japan. The Japanese began to appreciate their own folk culture and celebrate the beauty of the simple and understated. They embraced a sense of aesthetics based on outward simplicity and inner depth. Does this sound familiar? It should. You see it in the plain, unadorned white *keikogi* (uniform) you now wear to the *dojo*. You see it in the beauty of a faded and ragged black belt. It is why traditional karateka reject flashy uniforms, shiny belts with fancy embroidery, dojo decorated with all sorts of trinkets, and *kata* that have no practical application. Traditional karateka have absorbed an appreciation for the quiet, simple and functional owing to Yanagi and his artistic movement. And as we have seen, Yanagi drew his inspiration from Korea.

The beauty of the folk art Yanagi admired comes from the functionality of the object. There is no self-conscious effort on the part of the craftsman to make his bowl beautiful. He wants to make a good bowl. The beauty emerges because of his intent toward functionality. Likewise, the karateka understands that the beauty of a kata exists not because the practitioner is consciously trying to look good but because he applies himself to the meaning and function of the kata.

Practitioners of Japanese karate who disparage the Korean arts are ignorant of the fact that at least some of the aesthetics that guide karate have Korean roots. Koreans vehemently deny their Japanese roots, ignorant of the fact that their culture made considerable contributions to those roots. Life certainly can be ironic.

# DOES KATA PRACTICE PREPARE YOU FOR COMBAT?

*September 2000*

If you must go toe-to-toe with a beast, the straw tiger is a good one to fight. While he may have a fierce countenance, you can tip him over with the slightest effort.

Straw tigers came to mind as I was reading a new book on karate. The chapter devoted to *kata* was primarily about winning competitions. The author offered advice on musical kata and various gimmicks to gain the attention of officials. There was also a mention, almost smirking in tone, of "traditional kata." The author explained that many traditionalists consider kata to be "sacred," fixed forever in their current incarnations and copied endlessly in robotic form by slavish imitators.

The author compared the absurdity of traditional kata to the paintings of the great European masters: Wonderful as those paintings are, would anyone be happy just imitating the masters' work?

Well, no, I wouldn't. But what if someone offered to teach me all the technical secrets the masters used, all the tricks they knew for establishing composition, perspective and spatial arrangement? Would I be interested in learning that? You bet I would.

That is exactly what is taught through traditional kata training. The masters who developed and refined kata did not want them to be sterile masterpieces, imitated forever with no creative input, nor were they designed to teach the practicalities of combat. They were designed to teach at an instinctive level the principles of combat, body dynamics, timing, power, balance and motion that can make the practitioner more adaptable to a wide range of combat contingencies. Kata is not combat, but understanding kata permits us to meet combative situations with the proper skills.

My point is that the author grossly misrepresented kata and used that misrepresentation as proof that kata are worthless. It's like saying, "All people from Chicago beat their children. Therefore, I dislike the people of Chicago." The conclusion is absurd because the initial premise is absurd. The author blundered further when he asserted that unnamed traditionalists consider kata "sacred." Which traditionalists? None I know of. Yet by caricaturing these traditionalists as a herd of myopic geezers blindly worshipping some ritualized movements from the past, all those who practice kata are made to seem ridiculous.

Does the author have any grasp of the significance kata plays in a traditional *karateka's* maturation? I doubt it. The book extols the virtue of show business-type effects to dress up a kata "performance." Offered as validity for this cheesy notion is a list of traditionalists who have supposedly done just that. The message is: If even those stuffy old dinosaurs are doing it, it's got to be OK, right? Maybe. The only problem is that, of the seven or eight individuals cited, none could remotely be thought of as a traditionally trained karateka by others of that class. This kind of argument, in fact, is a tactic related to tackling straw tigers: "Master Joe Schmuck is the highest-ranked expert in the solar system, and he says building calluses on your nose is good. So nose calluses must be good." Of course, once again, the premise is faulty. Joe's actually a self-promoted yahoo. Whatever advice he has for you might accidentally be correct, but citing him as proof of its reliability is meaningless.

What causes people to construct these tigers of straw, label them as "traditional karate" and proceed to whack away? One reason is that the profundities, challenges and subtleties of karate as it has traditionally been practiced in Okinawa and Japan are quite intimidating—especially to small minds. Suspecting that they can never penetrate to its deeper levels, these people are driven to denigrate the art. They're a lot like Aesop's fox, who proclaimed the grapes sour only because he couldn't reach the clusters on the vine.

Another reason is that traditional karate, influenced by Okinawan culture and later by the aesthetics of Japanese *budo*, has scant use for big egos, pretension or silly displays of superficial power. And, needless to say, it is precisely these factors that draw some misguided individuals to the art in the first place; one assumes he can become "somebody" because he'll have the means and opportunity to display his new skills, but in the traditional *dojo*, he is met with hard work, attitudes that elevate humility into an art form, and the realization that he is merely one of many other beginners. Faced with these unpleasant truths, it's not surprising that many flee the harsh life of the dojo and seek refuge in the tawdry ghetto of pseudo-karate.

It would be OK if these people were content to perform their musical kata, parade about in their outlandish uniforms and confine themselves to the shallow circles where they belong. But when they venture out to criticize the real thing, when they misrepresent the tiger of karate with straw imitations, they need to be reminded that the real thing has teeth and claws and, if provoked, is apt to fight back.

# KEEPING KARATE IN PROPER PERSPECTIVE

*November 2000*

When I was a schoolboy during the 1960s, I spent a lot of my weekends rock climbing in the Ozarks with my friends. We'd occasionally run into others who shared our interest, and we'd sometimes run into fanatics.

We called them "climb *kichigai*" (climb crazy). They did not pursue climbing as an activity or a sport. For them, it was an obsession. These were the sort of guys who skipped weddings and funerals to go climbing.

It shouldn't be surprising that the *budo* have their own contingent of kichigai. Typically—but not always—they are young, male and can be spotted instantly by an intense, white-hot drive to train. Often they will be taped in half a dozen places to mark the injuries they've suffered. But they will still be at the *dojo* for every class, and they are apt to remain there long after everyone else has gone. These budo kichigai are frequently held up as models for other students to follow.

"Look at Joe-*san* over there," a teacher will remark with some pride. "Arm's broken and his mother died yesterday, but he just quit his job at the supermarket so he'll have more time to train."

And over there is indeed Joe, whacking away at a *makiwara*, a beatific look of joy adorning his sweaty face. You look at Joe and try to remember

---

The *sensei* will show him that the *dojo* is merely a training ground for life, and the lessons which apply in the dojo must—if they have any meaning or value—be worthwhile in situations outside the school.

---

where you've seen a similar expression—a face lit with that kind of inner light. And then it occurs to you that you've seen that expression in religious art. Saints smile like that.

So do idiots.

There may be a few saints among the budo kichigai. I suspect, however, that most are just plain idiots. That may sound harsh, but it's been my experience that many dojo fanatics are anything but worthy role models. While we train for the wider perspectives of life, their practice is an end in itself. They mistake the dojo for real life. Their training becomes a substitute for the interactions, responsibilities and relationships that real life imposes and promises.

A good *sensei* will point out the folly of the fanatic's attitude and approach to training. The sensei will show him that the dojo is merely a training ground for life, and the lessons which apply in the dojo must—if they have any meaning or value—be worthwhile in situations outside the school. True, punching the makiwara a couple hundred times a day doesn't have much relevance in daily life. The determination and consistency of that kind of practice, though, is instrumental in tackling challenges far removed from the confines of the dojo—things like keeping a steady job or finishing college.

More important, the teacher will point out to the budo kichigai that he is neglecting obligations and depending on others to take care of him. Look behind the fanatic and you will probably see a long-suffering spouse or parent footing the bills. They will be feeding him and taking care of his clothing, insurance, transportation and so on. He thinks his training is too important to be distracted by considerations of gratitude—or anything else at all.

The budo kichigai will rationalize: "Look at all I am giving up in order to train." In reality, it's those around him who are doing the giving. He is only taking. And that amounts to pure selfishness.

Training in the dojo is an essential part of the martial artist's search for a more meaningful life. If he approaches that training as a substitute for life, however, his reward will not be at all what he expects. There is no self-perfection at the end of that road, only a bitter and meaningless existence.

# THE BENEFITS OF JUDO

*December 2000*

Judo is not the same today as it was 30 or 40 years ago. Succumbing to the perhaps inevitable allure of sporting competition, it is now—with few exceptions—little more than a mildly effective form of wrestling. Enthusiasts who came to the *budo* after this devolution, however, should know something about the qualities judo once offered ... and still could. They might be inspired to follow it—if they can find one of the few places where it is still properly pursued. More likely, they might gain some valuable insight into how an art like judo can instill some core attitudes and values that will take them far into other arts they may choose to study.

"*Judoka* have a self-confidence that I've never seen in any other martial artist," I once heard a senior practitioner say. "That's because judo is one of the only arts that allows a person to see what he really can and can't do."

Consider the following: An *aikido* practitioner masters the *kote gaeshi*, a throw in which the wrist is reversed until the opponent is sent flying. Only it would never work that way. Kote gaeshi, in reality, could very well drop a person and dislocate his wrist, elbow and shoulder. But unless the person was well-trained in aikido, he wouldn't take that big fall. He'd go down in a screaming heap, almost certainly putting the mass of his weight in a direction with which the aikido practitioner has never had to contend.

---

**When you think about it, the *judoka* is unique because he can practice his techniques at full force and at full speed against an opponent who is fighting back with the same energy and intent.**

---

The aikido practitioner, in other words, can never practice his technique against an opponent for real.

The *karateka* suffers the same limitations. He may have practiced his reverse punch for 30 years, but has he ever uncorked it against a person who didn't want to be hit and was trying to hit him back at the same time? Probably not.

When you think about it, the judoka is unique because he can practice his techniques at full force and at full speed against an opponent who is fighting back with the same energy and intent. When a judoka drops his partner with a *harai goshi* (sweeping hip throw), he knows the technique

109

works. He knows what happens to his opponent during the movement, how he falls and what it feels like. This knowledge provides a lot of awareness about up-close fighting, and it encourages a realistic view of what one can and cannot do in a real situation. It also explains why martial artists who have gone on to other arts and haven't practiced judo for many years will instinctively use judo under the duress of an actual attack.

You might argue that the judoka does not have to deal with strikes. He may have practiced half a century and never taken a hard punch to the mouth. True. But the same could be said of most karateka. When they do take blows, it is nearly always accidental. It might hurt, but it doesn't feel like someone's taking a deliberate shot.

Critics also observe that founder Jigoro Kano took all the dangerous parts out of *jujutsu* when he developed judo. There's something to that. There's no question that he did away with certain joint locks, nerve strikes and other aspects of classical or modern jujutsu. We are talking, however, about the sensation of trying to control and physically dominate another person who is trying to do the same to you. Part of the great genius of Kano was that he created an art that allowed for a considerably broad range of realistic attacks and responses. Correctly practiced, judo offers an interplay of offense and defense that requires an acknowledgment of rules on both sides, but it also permits a broad exploration of more or less realistic combat.

It's interesting, too, that judoka rarely have the exaggerated sense of their own "deadliness" that you see in karate practitioners—or the romanticized sense of self that one sees in aikido practitioners who believe they can effortlessly "blend" with any attack and neutralize it. I suspect that judoka have a more realistic concept of themselves and their combative abilities for the simple reason that they've thrown and have been thrown, choked and have been choked so often that there is little room for misconception.

It's too bad that judo has degenerated. It's too bad that more young martial artists are not able to get a foundation in it the way it used to be practiced before they branch out into other arts. I'm convinced that, if they did, they'd be better off for the experience.

# A SINGLE SHOT

*March 2001*

In his book *Tsure-zure-gusa*, or "Essays of Idle Grasses" (ca. 1330), Kenko Yoshida takes on a subject that is familiar to all martial warriors: *ichi-gi ichi-e*, or "one encounter, one chance." To illustrate his point, Kenko cites the following example:

"A warrior, when he was practicing the drawing of his bow, faced the target with two arrows in his left hand. Observing this, the instructor said, 'Beginners must not have two arrows in the hand because, since they count on the second, they always become careless when they aim at the target with the first. Therefore, you ought to think every time you draw an arrow, to hit with it alone.' This advice is applicable for all matters. Those who wish to study instead talk into the night of the weather the next morning, the next day about the weather for the afternoon—they are delayed in this manner. We always have a project, and we must work to give immediate satisfaction to our intention."

The Japanese arts, especially the fighting arts, are deeply interwoven with the concept that one must approach every endeavor with the mentality that there is but a single chance. Indeed, ichi-gi ichi-e has a deep resonance in Japanese culture. Consider the art of calligraphy. The briefest touch

---

**Many Westerners are fascinated by the "one encounter, one chance" philosophy because it resonates with the central theme of Christian theology, in which we are reminded that we have but one life, one chance.**

---

of a brush to paper produces a mark that cannot be erased. You have to live with what you have put on the paper, good or bad. The art of flower arrangement celebrates this concept, stressing the idea that one has but a fleeting moment to arrange blossoms beautifully before they wither. Similarly, the way of tea reminds participants there is but "one encounter, one chance" to enjoy the steaming bowl that sits before them. The season, the fellowship of the tea hut, and the skill of the preparer all will change, even if the ceremony is repeated the very next day.

Ichi-gi ichi-e particularly resonates in the *budo*, probably because of the nature of the *katana*, which is not conducive to quick ripostes or follow-up strikes. You get one chance: Miss it, and you die. The expression *ikken*

THE BEST OF DAVE LOWRY

*hisatsu,* "killing with one strike," is a martial version of ichi-gi ichi-e.

Many Westerners are fascinated by the "one encounter, one chance" philosophy because it resonates with the central theme of Christian theology, in which we are reminded that we have but one life, one chance. However, confronting this concept presents some problems for the budo practitioner in general and for the karate practitioner in particular. While many budo practitioners assume that all fighters believe, "I've got one chance in this fight to live or die," in reality this is not always the case. If you watch a good Philippine knife fighter in action, you will see that his tactics include quick little cuts, much like those of a European fencer. He plans to win not with a single decisive blow but through an accumulation of blood loss as cut after cut gradually wears the opponent down. Many Chinese combative arts teach a series of attacks that are unleashed in quick succession. Block or evade the first, and the second is already on its way.

The karate practitioner gets caught somewhere in the middle of these contrasting philosophies of combat. There is no need to argue about which strategy is more effective. You must simply understand that they exist and that, in training and in real-life situations, it is unrealistic to expect everyone to play by your strategic rules.

# RECEIVING THE ATTACK

*May 2001*

Miyako Obata—whose husband, Isao Obata, is one of the great Japanese *karateka* of the postwar era—once told a tale about an incident that occurred in 1935. The Japanese had occupied Manchuria, and Isao was working there as an adviser for an airplane manufacturer. One night, the couple was out for a stroll when Isao attempted to break up a street-corner argument. Someone threw a punch at him, and as his wife tells it, he blocked the attack and "the assailant just disappeared. [He] flew completely over a car that was parked along the street."

This anecdote illustrates the power of a strong *uke waza*, or blocking technique. Unfortunately, such technique is extremely hard to develop. If you want to perfect your strikes, you can always hit a *makiwara* or heavy bag; but to polish blocking methods, you need a live partner, one you can trust to measure his attacks exactly to your ability. Too light a strike, and you don't improve your blocking technique; too strong, and you get your lights put out.

Once you manage to find a partner you can trust, I suggest the following method of training: Have your partner throw a right step-in punch to

---

**Learning to avoid an attack by shifting your body and hands will give you greater freedom and mobility to counter, even when you do use your arms to block.**

---

your chest. Stand in a front stance and block the punch with a left *soto uke* (outer forearm block that travels across your body from left to right). You are probably familiar with this exchange; in one-step sparring, it is followed by a right reverse punch. Don't worry about the counterpunch here, though. Just execute the block a few times. Then have him punch again, and try to avoid the punch with the body movement of the block. No arm motion, just shift your body.

If you've never done this before, you will find that it can teach you a whole lot very quickly. First, you'll see that the basic method of soto uke, in which your feet don't move at all and your arms do much of the work, is not effective. You must shift your entire stance. You will probably have shifted fractionally to your left. This action is called *yori ashi*.

Second, you'll discover that timing is crucial. When you were making a comparatively wide sweeping block, you could encounter the incoming punch at many places in its course and still successfully brush it aside. Shifting and avoiding with your body alone means there is a very small window of opportunity for effective movement.

Third, it should become obvious that a very sharp hip twist is all that will protect your chest. If you are practicing good karate, you will have had

this hip motion and twisting preached to you from your first class. Now you will begin to see what it really means.

Most important, you should learn that the motion of your arms in blocking is not the essential movement. Moving your body center is. Learning to avoid an attack by shifting your body and hands will give you greater freedom and mobility to counter, even when you do use your arms to block. The block—and this is a poor translation of *uke*, which is more accurately described as "to accept"—is a way of redirecting the attack once it has been negated.

Beginners have difficulty understanding this last point. They tend to use too much arm and shoulder strength when they block, trying to knock the attack off course. This works, provided the blocking arm or the person behind it is physically stronger than the attacker. Consider: If someone throws a pillow at you, you can stand your ground and knock it aside. But if you try the same tactic with a 250-pound guy barreling at you on a mountain bike, you won't be able to push him aside because he has too much momentum and too much mass for you to confront head-on. Instead, you must shift and step to the side, and from that angle a relatively light push will send him careening out of control. This is the real concept behind karate's uke waza.

The ability to knock an attacker over a car with a block may be beyond the grasp of most of us. But by practicing properly, you will be surprised at how much stronger and more efficient your blocking techniques can be.

# ULTIMATE GOAL OF KARATE TRAINING

*June 2001*

If the subject of the best *karateka* in the world today were brought up, how long would the discussion last before Hirokazu Kanazawa were mentioned? His name is instantly familiar to any serious martial artist and conjures up a sense of respect that borders on awe—especially among those who have seen him in person. Kanazawa, a 10th-degree black belt and chief of Shotokan Karate International, is unquestionably one of the world's most skilled practitioners.

Kanazawa began his training with the Japan Karate Association after World War II. His seniors and teachers included Hidetaka Nishiyama, Teruyuki Okazaki and the late Masatoshi Nakayama. In 1967, Kanazawa entered the All-Japan Karate Championships, and despite the fact that he had a broken hand and had never even trained in free-sparring for competition, he won. His tournament record has never been equaled, leading *Black Belt* in 1983 to label him the greatest karate fighter of all time. Kanazawa was among the first generation of karateka to graduate from the fabled Japan Karate Association instructors' training program. Since then, he has taught his art on every populated continent in the world and oversees the karate education of hundreds of thousands of students globally.

Kanazawa did not reach this level of expertise easily. During his early training, he punched and kicked in endless repetition, day after day, year after year, until his body became a mass of sinewy armor. Today, even his simplest movements reveal his extraordinary level of skill. He sometimes gives the impression that he's able to glide above the ground in fluid motion and then, at the focus of a technique, he looks to be rooted inseparably from it. The force of his kicks reverberates in the air around him.

By any standard, Kanazawa is a formidably strong man. He possesses the physical strength for which our culture has always afforded respect. Just as famous athletes inspire their fans and followers, Kanazawa and the other *budo* experts are a source of admiration and emulation for martial artists all over the world. Those who have trained with *sensei* at Kanazawa's level will tell you that it is easy to become mesmerized by that kind of strength. They come to accept the idea that their teacher's strength is, for all practical purposes, invincible.

Traditional karate training, however, does not follow the same regimen as sports, nor are its goals similar. Yes, karateka try very hard to make their muscles more efficient and improve their cardiovascular endurance; in short, they work just like any athlete to be stronger. But far more important to the karateka is the development of inner strength, or *damashi*.

*Budo no damashi*, the "spirit of the martial ways," is something that transcends the limited capabilities of the body. It is the part of the karateka's personality that is not immediately evident, the part that is molded by long hours spent practicing the basics and fortifying the spirit, and by the even longer hours spent learning an advanced *kata* that will take a decade of work before he even begins to understand its movements. Damashi is nurtured by the courage necessary to face a vastly superior opponent in a match—not with the hope of winning but of gaining some insight from the encounter. It is a refined sort of toughness that cannot be acquired through cursing at a football coach or a martial arts teacher. Rather, damashi is an attribute attained through an intensely individual commitment to the martial way, the ultimate aim of which is the perfection of the self. In talented and dedicated practitioners, damashi eventually spills over from their practice and influences their everyday life, allowing them to successfully meet the challenges of life with the same calm determination with which they approach challenges in the *dojo*.

Damashi is a subtle strength, discernible only to more advanced students who have at least started their own journey toward achieving it. Even so, it is unquestionably one of the characteristics that separate the budo from sports. Damashi is one of the vital criteria that distinguishes Kanazawa and other experts in karate, judo, *aikido* and *kendo* from other athletes. Even if Kanazawa became disabled and could not practice the physical techniques of karate again, through the patiently developed fortitude of damashi, he would continue to be a worthwhile human being, at peace with himself and the world. Even though his physical power is transient, just as it is with all of us, Kanazawa's damashi will remain throughout his life, allowing him to live with grace and dignity.

The techniques of karate as performed by its greatest experts inspire awe in the rest of us, and rightfully so. They are observed at every opportunity and copied as faithfully as possible in our own practice. But karateka—especially those who are young and healthy and bursting with energy and enthusiasm—should never forget that physical skill and ability are tools. They are important for building a body strong enough to practice karate. Yet energy and enthusiasm are more necessary for creating the damashi that will sustain them long after an accident, illness or age has ebbed their strength.

# OKINAWAN TERMINOLOGY

*July 2001*

If a practitioner of Japanese karate wants to learn the technical lexicon of his art, he can find numerous books and other sources that contain extensive vocabularies. Followers of Okinawan karate, however, frequently contact me, wondering what it's called when they do this or that. One problem is that the language of Okinawa is filled with dialects and idiosyncrasies that differ from region to region. This is hard to imagine on a tiny group of islands, but like Japan, Okinawa has historically been a collection of separate communities with little interaction. The language reflects this fact, and terms used by one karate teacher as recently as 50 years ago might not have been used the same way, or even understood, by a teacher in the next village.

Another problem is that, although many words in *hogan* (the language of Okinawa) are clearly borrowed from Japanese, they sometimes have a very different meaning. For example, the Okinawan word *yaware* means virtually the same thing as the Japanese *yawara*. Both mean "pliant" or "flexible." But while *kearu* is often translated as the Okinawan equivalent of the Japanese word *ki*, the two are not the same and cannot be used the same way.

That said, let's look at some of the more common words used in Okinawan karate, specifically those used in the practice of *kata*. A fundamental

---

**Terms used by one karate teacher as recently as 50 years ago might not have been used the same way, or even understood, by a teacher in the next village.**

---

precept of kata is that they demonstrate a harmony between *ijiki* and *soyora*. The former means "spirited" or "full of power" and the latter means "softly" or "gently." If a kata has moments and movements that strike a balance of these, it is said to be *shinate*—"harmonious" or "well-adjusted." A common complaint of the older Okinawan masters regarding kata today—especially the kata performed by Japanese practitioners—is that there is too much ijiki and not enough soyora. The ijiki, they say, is like a thunderstorm: We all notice it. But the soyora represents the atmospheric conditions that allow the storm to develop in the first place—not so obvious but vital.

Repeated movements like the three successive strikes or blocks found in the *pinan* or *heian* kata, if done correctly, have the quality of *tsuri*, which is most often heard in Okinawan as *nami-tsuriyose* and refers to the prow of a boat plowing through the waves with a strong, steady beat. When you perform certain moves in kata, you have this same sense of driving through a series of waves.

You will frequently see *karateka* go from one kata technique to the next, hurrying along without giving the first movement the proper emphasis. These techniques lack *keyagetoru*, an Okinawan word used to describe actions that is decisively completed. I have been told it comes from two Japanese words: *keage* and *toru*. Keage, as most Japanese karateka know, means "to kick upward." Toru means "to take" or "to do." And so the word supposedly refers to the decisive action of kicking. Nonsense, one Okinawan karateka said. It comes from the Japanese *kenage*, meaning "manly" or "ideally masculine." Since I have heard this term used by Okinawans who know nothing of karate—which implies that it is not strictly related to combat—I wonder which theory is closer to the truth.

*Ibuki* is what the Japanese call the particular method of breathing in some kata. In Okinawan, it's *ibuche*. *Uchiche* means "to hit," a word almost certainly derived from the Japanese *uchi*. But Okinawan has a unique variation, *uchichiesu*, which means specifically "to strike in such a way that the opponent is completely defeated." In other words, it is the finishing blow.

*Umuiri* is another unique Okinawan term frequently heard during discussions about kata. It's difficult to translate directly; perhaps the best way is "inner beauty." It's used to describe a karateka who has so thoroughly integrated the movements of the form that his own, distinctive personality begins to emerge from it. According to the old masters, this is when the true "art" of karate becomes evident. If a person is cruel, self-centered or malicious, he can still perfect the physical techniques of karate. But what will eventually surface in the performance of his kata will be those flaws. Only if he is a good and worthwhile person at the center of his being will umuiri reveal itself.

Some of those older Okinawans insist that it's impossible to understand their karate without having knowledge of their language. Even the Japanese, they say, have missed many of the nuances of Okinawan karate because they do not have words that correctly describe the art's essence. When you consider terms like *umuiri*, you realize they may have a point.

# REACHING THE TARGET
*August 2001*

The *kyudoka* (practitioner of Japanese archery) distinguishes three ways of hitting a target with his shot. They may all look the same and the arrow may end up in precisely the same spot on the target, but they are very different. The ways in which the archer hits the target are not so different from the ways we who practice other forms of the *budo* hit our own targets.

*Toteki* is the term for the shot that makes it to the target accurately. It does not matter how it gets there, only that it does. The archer's form may be poor and his shot may be a matter of luck more than skill, but that doesn't matter. What counts is that the arrow got to the target and hit it in the right spot.

Professional athletes, for the most part, strive for a toteki approach to competition. They don't care how good their team looked; they care only that they scored more points than their opponents. A person in danger

---

**[Martial arts'] methods are simply to engage in a series of movements that are performed with such commitment to perfection that they go to the limits of physical skill and beyond.**

---

might also adopt this mentality: I don't care how good I look getting away from the guy with the gun; I just want to get away.

If you shoot an arrow and your teacher corrects your form, you might say, "But look, I hit the target."

"Yes," he will tell you, "but if you want to hit it consistently and not just as the result of luck, you need to correct this or that." If you follow his advice, you leave the realm of toteki and go to *kanteki*.

The archer who "penetrates" the target is said to be shooting kanteki. The term refers to a target that is hit convincingly, deliberately and reliably. Law-enforcement officers are a good example of this mentality. For example, if they have a confrontation with a belligerent motorist they've stopped for reckless driving, they must control the situation authoritatively. They must "win" not by accident or lucky happenstance but in a way that can be repeated and that does as little damage as possible to the driver, since the officer will undoubtedly encounter this kind of situation again.

In the old days of Japan when archery was a martial art that was actually

used on the battlefield, kanteki was the aim of the archer. His attention to form was critical, not because it made him look good but because it was the surest way to successfully deliver an arrow into an enemy.

Kanteki is pure practicality, the highest level of physical skill. For some, this is sufficient. For others, there is something more, something beyond just the physical. For them, if they have the fortitude and a competent guide, the realm of *zaiteki* beckons.

With zaiteki, the archer is no longer hitting the target. Rather, he has, in a metaphysical sense, "become" the target. Zaiteki marks the point at which a martial art is elevated into a moral, ethical and spiritual way. At this point, it's easy to start indulging in a lot of New Age babble, but the martial ways are not that sort of thing. They are classical in nature—deeply so—and they would reject a lot of mystical mumbo-jumbo. Their methods are simply to engage in a series of movements that are performed with such commitment to perfection that they go to the limits of physical skill and beyond. Getting to that place is the process of discovering zaiteki.

The person who reads an article on self-defense, then goes out that very day and is attacked and defends himself, is successful. But it's toteki—more luck than anything else. The person who practices the physical movements of karate for 30 years may have adequate resources to defend himself against attacks even if they come on a regular basis. He is like the archer at the stage of kanteki. The person who pushes past this stage and continues to pursue karate into its higher realms hits the target at the level of zaiteki. From the outside they may look alike, but in truth they are quite different.

# DEAR SENSEI

*October 2001*

Your *sensei* does not know everything. Sorry to be so blunt, but it's a fact you really ought to consider. I'm not saying he isn't qualified to teach you karate. I'm referring to his ability to give advice on other things—like your love life, your career or your efforts to stop smoking.

Of course, he might be able to offer some very good advice on these or other personal matters. You know and trust him, so it's reasonable for you to seek him out if you need some counseling or just want someone to listen. In this sense, a karate teacher is like anyone else with whom you want to talk. But keep this in mind: Your karate teacher has not gone to "sensei school" where he took classes in how to help people solve personal problems or make decisions. He is probably very wise in the art of karate, but his insights into whom you ought to marry or which school you ought to apply to next fall is probably no different from what your parents, a minister or a therapist might tell you. Remember, too, that in most cases, while these latter people will give you their opinion, they do not presume to give advice when you have not asked for it.

I mention all this because for some reason a lot of martial arts teachers believe they have some special abilities beyond the teaching of the art. They

---

**It is critical to avoid falling—or being led—into the trap of letting your instructor make decisions for you that you ought to make for yourself.**

---

behave as if they almost have a duty to counsel their students in all sorts of personal areas of their lives. I've heard of sensei telling students that they should marry a certain person, seek a divorce, put off their schooling or find a different job. I'm astounded that the students act as though the sensei had some legal or moral authority over them, but I suppose it's understandable in some respects.

There are two reasons why sensei behave this way. The first has to do with the way in which we have perennially approached sports in the West. Beginning with the Greeks, we have considered sports to be analogous to, and a training ground for, real life. Sports teach us to be gracious winners and stoic losers, and they teach teamwork and virtue. So it's hardly remarkable that we regard the authority figure in sports—the coach—as a kind of

Aristotelian mentor and father figure. It is not a stretch at all for the sensei to be perceived as a coach. The sensei not only teaches the technical aspects of his art but also guides his students in a deeper understanding of life. When you treat a person this way, it isn't surprising that he acts the part. If you put him in the same category as a coach—often interacting with athletes who are younger and less experienced in life than he is—he will take on the responsibilities you appear to be expecting of him.

Second, there is a lot of Oriental mysticism that surrounds the sensei. He is Mr. Miyagi and Yoda and that blind guy who was David Carradine's master on *Kung Fu*. He is all-knowing. He has all the answers. If he can teach you, if he can give you the self-confidence to put your fist through a stack of boards, is it too much to believe that he knows whether you and your spouse should have kids?

It's not merely the students' beliefs about their teacher that builds this aura of the sensei as Ann Landers. If he is unscrupulous, he can also promote it. It's very enjoyable to tell other people what to do and how to run their lives. It's also a way of reinforcing their status and sense of self. The sensei's image among his students is enhanced by his role as an advice-giver, and being consulted about personal matters gives him more power. A sensei that is indispensable for making decisions about areas of your life gains control over you that extends far beyond the hours you spend under his tutelage in the *dojo*.

This is rarely a healthy situation for you, your teacher or the other students at the dojo. The *karateka* is supposed to expand his sense of self and control over his own life. It is the sensei's job to guide this growth. When he exerts his own control over the student, he is working toward precisely the opposite goal.

It is critical to avoid falling—or being led—into the trap of letting your instructor make decisions for you that you ought to make for yourself. You must recognize the signs. You must acknowledge the natural human tendency to let others make hard decisions for you instead of confronting them yourself. You must expect and demand to be treated as a student and not as a child or a ward. If you cannot take responsibility for your own life, you have no business trying to follow the way of karate. If your teacher cannot give you that responsibility, he has no business trying to lead you there.

# A CHALLENGE TO THE MASTERS

*February 2002*

Almost every month, *Black Belt* receives at least one letter from some-one claiming to be a master. These people write to offer comments or (more likely) criticism on a wide range of subjects. They also recommend the magazine publish articles about them, extolling the virtues of their sundry seminars and clinics and videos—a very thoughtful and generous gesture on their part. In particular, *Black Belt* hears from "masters" after an article is published suggesting that one of them might not be a master, exactly, but rather a pretentious jackass.

From all the mail that is received, I would estimate that any city large enough to have a Wal-Mart also has at least one martial arts master. That leaves me with a question: If there are so many masters running around, how come we have so few masterpieces?

Yes, I wrote "masterpieces." Isn't that what masters are supposed to produce? Bach was a master musician; he composed masterworks like his "Brandenberg Concertos." Botticelli was a master painter, and anyone who has seen *The Birth of Venus* will attest to it. There are museums full of paintings and sculptures, and concert halls brimming with great music. These are the representations of the masters who generated them. They

---

**Instead of offering to beat people up, how about creating something of value, something of beauty, something worthy of emulation?**

---

are, in a sense, the proof of the mastery of the authors. That is true, you may argue, but the martial arts are different from the fine arts. Not so.

Traditional martial arts masters have created an array of masterpieces in their time. Some of these works would fall into the category of art, as we're accustomed to thinking of it. For instance, the legendary swordsman Miyamoto Musashi carved wooden sculptures, forged magnificent hand guards for swords and painted the illustrations that you may have seen in his texts. The Hotokuji Temple in Nara Prefecture has numerous examples of the ink paintings and calligraphy done by masters of the *Shinkage-ryu*. The fencing master Yagyu Renyasai is as famous for his beautifully crafted hand guards as he is for his fighting ability. Yamaoka Tesshu, one of the most famous swordsmen of the early 19th century, is also regarded as one of the finest calligraphers of Japan.

Modern *budo* masters have, in many cases, continued this artistic tradition. Judo founder Jigoro Kano and *shotokan's* Gichin Funakoshi were both calligraphers and poets of considerable skill. So was *aikido's* Morihei Uyeshiba. In addition to these examples in the fine arts, the masters of the budo crafted other masterpieces. While we may not think of them as such, the students they left behind are living proof of their genius. In spite of the travails of early modern Japan—a disastrous militarization and an even more devastating war—the mastery of Kano, Funakoshi and Uyeshiba prevailed and produced *budoka* who have illuminated our generation: Kyuzo Mifune, Kisshomaru Uyeshiba and Masatoshi Nakayama.

All of this brings us to my original question: Where are the masterpieces made by all the masters who are cluttering up the countryside? I suppose we might have a half-dozen of the current crop who've had roles in films. Some have penned technical how-to manuals or largely self-serving narratives. But would these people have us believe such products are the equivalent of the masterpieces from previous generations? I think not.

Recently, it has become fashionable for some of these masters to issue challenges. They offer cash rewards to anyone willing to take them on. Others dare famous boxers to meet them in the ring. This is an old and tired publicity ploy, since the well-known boxer has nothing to gain by KO'ing a nobody—and for the vast majority of masters, "nobody" is a perfect description.

Well, I have a challenge of my own I would like to issue to these masters and all the others who are thinking of having that title printed on their stationery. Simply put, I challenge them to produce some masterpieces. Instead of offering to beat people up, how about creating something of value, something of beauty, something worthy of emulation? If you're really a master, you should be able to produce a student of the caliber turned out by another master. You should be able to mold and shape someone.

So how about it, Master Knucklehead? Are you up to the task, or is this a challenge that's just too dangerous for even you to take on?

127

# PRACTICING WRONG

*May 2002*

Martial artists speak of the essential elements for polishing *kata*—things like spirit, focus, rhythm and timing—but another quality is often overlooked: the willingness to do the kata wrong.

As odd as that may sound, it is an important part of perfecting a kata. Of course, "perfecting" is a subjective concept. The perfect rendition of a kata done by a competent brown belt with five years of training under that belt will look good. It won't, however, look anything like that of a fifth-*dan* black belt with 30 or 40 years of training. The perfect kata is actually something that can occur only within the mind of the individual practitioner. If it is done to the best of his inner estimation, then no matter what it may have looked like to others, the kata is arguably perfect for him.

But it's pointless to think in terms of perfection; it's much better to continue to try to improve—no matter what your level. The most common way to move toward that goal is to envision an absolutely correct, flawless model. And that can be a problem.

As something of a perfectionist, I often go to the *dojo* with that picture in my mind, that image of those *karateka* whose form I admire. To some extent, I practice to look like them. And while I may train hard, when I see myself starting to look sloppy or lose my crispness and snap, I tend to

---

**Our best karate occurs not as a singular event but as a result of doing a lot of karate that isn't our best.**

---

stop and rest, to gather myself for another effort. That's a mistake. What I need to do is continue training even though I'm doing the kata so poorly that I am, in effect, doing it wrong.

I find myself averse to practicing techniques at less than 100 percent of what I'm capable of doing. When a technique starts to look sloppy, I want to stop so I am refreshed and able to perform the kick or punch to the best of my ability. I'm willing to bet that most who are serious about karate or any other *budo* are the same.

What we need to keep in mind is that a lot of progress comes when we do things wrong. I'm not talking about doing things wrong deliberately, so perhaps that's not the right word. But we need to practice techniques when they don't have that edge and crispness about them. We need to do them even though they aren't our best.

It's easy to misunderstand this attitude. Does it mean we should go to the dojo and just go through the motions? Hardly. We have to put forth our best effort each time. We also have to recognize that our best isn't always going to be the same. It's easy to fall into the habit of saying, "If I can't do it perfectly, I'd rather not do it at all." That's a convenient position to take because it excuses us from training in a lot of situations: "I'm not skipping practice this evening because I'm lazy or want to do something else. Nope, I'm skipping practice because I'm so noble and so serious about my karate that I refuse to be sloppy and halfway involved."

Yeah, right. Adopt that attitude and you'll eventually see your ability rapidly diminish. Before long, you'll be telling yourself, "I think I'll just wait until next summer, and then I can get back into it for real."

Our best karate occurs not as a singular event but as a result of doing a lot of karate that isn't our best. This is frustrating, I know, and it's a foreign idea for us. But if we want to perfect our karate, we must be willing to do it wrong.

# THE "SAMURAI WAY"

*June 2002*

The typical *karateka* tends to look at his teacher as a modern-day samurai—especially if that teacher is of Japanese ancestry. He sees military-type training as a contemporary counterpart to the apprenticeship undertaken by the feudal warriors of Japan.

Both suppositions are nonsense. Karate training today is only tangentially related to the methods of combat used by the samurai. The average 21st century karate teacher—Japanese or not—doesn't know spit from apple butter about the samurai.

A quick history lesson is in order. It seems reasonable to expect that the post-military force of Japan, the imperial army, drew its strength from the ranks of the samurai. In fact, many who descended from traditional samurai families viewed the army with considerable distaste and were less than thrilled with the thought of the "common folk" presuming to be

> It is culturally dishonest for *sensei* to present themselves as inheritors of a lifestyle to which they have no more an intimate connection than the average American has to a colonial rebel who fought at Lexington.

warriors. Consequently, most of the descendants of samurai stock enlisted in the Japanese navy, which had a far more aristocratic tradition than the army. During World War II, most Japanese soldiers were men whose ancestors had been farmers or merchants. What this means is that the imperial army officer you see in old newsreels swaggering and strutting with his sword dangling from his belt is far more likely to have been the grandson of a potato farmer than of a samurai.

Because the army had no warrior traditions of its own (there was no Japanese army before 1867), it had to create one. Understandably, it gravitated toward the aura of *bushido*—the "way of the warrior." But remember that the modern soldier had no experience with the mores and ethos of the samurai and was apt to hold their courage in awe. The military knew that exploiting this awe would work to its benefit, but it did not understand that the samurai's mentality developed from an evolution of complex societal pressures. The army hoped to attain those same ends through harsh physical conditioning, combining brutal exercises and incessant drills with sadistic discipline. Soldiers and officers were led to believe that this was the way the samurai had trained—a misconception they swallowed gladly—and they went on to *banzai*-charge their way into World War II by believing themselves to be the modern embodiment of a proud martial tradition.

The Japanese civilian population also gobbled up the "modern samurai" stuff. Male high-school students began wearing high-collar uniforms mod-

eled after those of the Prussian army. Martial songs were in vogue. Just as many Americans like to imagine their European ancestors as noble knights, the Japanese were encouraged to magnify and distort their memories of their ancestors: Your great-great-great-grandfather who was forced to leave his field and carry a spear in some inconsequential campaign instantly became a revered hero.

The *budo*, too, were used for this militaristic propaganda. Karate—particularly because it was a newcomer on the scene—readily adopted this approach, and the majority of Japanese karate teachers today are products of it. They continue to teach the way they learned, with an emphasis on shouting, military-type rigidity, discipline and so on.

So what? After all, the benefits of karate are outstanding. The excesses of the old military-style training have been abandoned, and the discipline and hardships that remain are excellent ways of learning. It may well be that the formal militarizing of karate is the best thing that ever happened to it. Karate is meant for people of all kinds, not just the samurai elite who studied battlefield combat. However, the tradition of military training in the *dojo* must be recognized for what it is. It is historically bogus to continue insisting that "Drop and gimme 20!" and *"Osu!"* shouted at every opportunity have any link with the training of the samurai. It is culturally dishonest for *sensei* to present themselves as inheritors of a lifestyle to which they have no more an intimate connection than the average American has to a colonial rebel who fought at Lexington. To continue this misconception is to keep alive the propaganda of a long-dead imperialistic mind-set and prevent us from seeing and following *karate-do* as it really is.

# THE WAY TO THE WAY

*August 2002*

When I was a kid, I was fortunate that both *dojo* where I trained were within walking distance of my home and school. I never considered it fortunate at the time, for it was quite a hike. But it was a walk through quiet streets lined with old trees, a beautiful park and a peaceful cemetery. Walking to practice, I would think about the latest technique or *kata*. Walking home, I tried to remember what I'd learned and the mistakes I'd made. But the real value of those walks lay in the moments they afforded me for contemplation and reflection. They gave me time to think about things my *sensei* had said or done.

On the way to the dojo after school, I had the opportunity to decompress the ennui, indignities and irritations that had been heaped on me that day. It separated the intensity of training from the comparative quiet of daily life—and sometimes just the opposite, when the training hall became a place of calm and refuge from the rest of my hectic life. The walks were a re-entry between two very different worlds. Unimportant as they may seem, my training would not have been the same without them.

Anyone who has participated in a formal tea ceremony in a structure built for that purpose within a specially designed garden understands

---

**It reminds me once again that, in matters such as the *budo*, what is important is not the destination but the journey itself.**

---

exactly what I'm talking about. Everything in the tea garden—plants, rocks, fences and so on—is placed for a specific effect. That includes the pathways that lead the participant to the room where the ceremony takes place. At the entrance to the tea garden, the pathways, usually paved with natural stones, are straight or gently curved. As you get closer, though, the path becomes more zigzagged. In garden architecture, these two paths are called *gan-kake* and *chidori-kake*. The first is named after the way a flock of geese flies across the sky: relatively straight, in a rhythmic pattern of wing beats. A *chidori* is a shorebird that darts back and forth along the sand, just like the path twists and turns. A chidori-kake has lots of bends, and its stones are unevenly spaced. Just as you have to slow down physically, you must slow down emotionally to prepare your mind for the contemplative process of the tea ceremony. I've always thought of a walk to the dojo as

working the same way, a far different method of approaching the training hall than hopping in the car and driving, then hopping out again and going directly inside.

Of course, in this frantic age, the journey to the training hall can be just one more rush we have to make. Scrambling from work or school, we may arrive at the dojo, dress and be on the training floor before we've had a chance to leave behind the problems and distractions of everyday life. Not surprisingly, and often to the detriment of our *budo* training, we carry those problems and their attendant emotions with us into practice. And going home afterward, how often are we in a similar hurry? When we are, we take the frustrations and supercharged emotions of the training hall with us.

There is a trip to a dojo near my home that in some ways is as pleasant as any I've made to a training hall. It leads to a karate club that meets at a rural community college about 40 miles away. It is surrounded by meadows and cornfields and rolling, wooded hills. As soon as I leave the city, the highway opens up. In the summer, the green all around instantly relaxes me. The heat of the day is replaced by the refreshing coolness of the country evening. In the winter, the landscape is somber and brown, and I drive in the deep dark, watching the moon as it comes up cold and white over the bare crests of the hills. Fall is the scent of wood smoke coming through the car window; spring is the smell of new-turned earth.

It is the trip there as much as the training that motivates me to finish dinner early, gas up the car and head out. The quiet and natural beauty along the way are a pleasant prelude and postlude to karate training, and I never take that way to the dojo without appreciating it. The trip slows me down. It focuses me and, at the same time, broadens my perspective on things. It reminds me once again that, in matters such as the budo, what is important is not the destination but the journey itself.

# TRAINING CAMPS
*September 2002*

A mericans love martial arts seminars. Pick up a copy of *Black Belt* and you will no doubt see dozens of advertisements for seminars of every kind. It's interesting to note that, while hundreds of such training events go on every year, practitioners in this country rarely hear about *gasshuku*.

Gasshuku are traditional martial arts training camps, and they are organized almost every month in Japan. In train stations all over the country, groups of people can be seen embarking for the mountains or the shore, their luggage packed with training uniforms and the tools of their art. They are bound for gasshuku to learn, train, test themselves and make or renew wonderful friendships.

Traditionally, gasshuku take place outdoors in the countryside. Imagine taking a weeklong camping trip with your karate class, and you'll begin to get the picture. For years, *goju-ryu* practitioners from Tokyo have traveled to the mountains around Kiso in Japan's central highlands for their gasshuku. Every year, the famous Tobukan *dojo* in Mito Prefecture hosts a children's gasshuku for its *kendo* classes near the Shinto shrine at Ise.

---

**The fifth-*dan* practices right beside the white belt, and it is very likely he'll be beside him peeling potatoes for dinner that evening, too.**

---

But there are also gasshuku on the buttes of South Africa, in the French countryside and on California beaches.

Unlike most seminars that present new material to participants, gasshuku usually concentrate on what has already been learned. What distinguishes gasshuku training is that the practice is often creative. On Mount Kiso, *karateka* drape watermelons over their shoulders in webbed slings and have a *kumite* free-for-all, with the winner being the last guy with his melons intact. Kendo gasshuku have a variation of this: Instead of melons, practitioners tie balloons to the foreheads of their masks.

Gasshuku at the seashore might include *kata* practice in the surf, going through the motions as waves suck in and out, toppling the unwary. Performing the same kata on a steep mountain slope gives a lot of insight into the meaning of stance and movement on uneven ground. A popular method at karate gasshuku involves a participant standing with his back to a riverbank, free-sparring with a series of opponents, each one intent on making him take a dive—literally. Another gasshuku exercise involves each participant "adopting" a basketball-size rock for the duration of the camp. The rock is carried on runs, during warm-ups and even to meals. After a couple days, more than a few participants come up with some interesting names for their charges.

In short, gasshuku exercises are limited only by the imagination of the senior organizers, and while they're mostly difficult and challenging, they're also a heck of a lot of fun.

One more distinction separates gasshuku from other seminars: The division between seniors and juniors and even teachers and students is often deliberately lowered. Seniors and teachers are always present, of course, but no "master" stands around and counts out movements or teaches formally. The fifth-*dan* practices right beside the white belt, and it is very likely he'll be beside him peeling potatoes for dinner that evening, too.

I once asked a gasshuku veteran what he liked best about these training camps. *"Bureiko,"* he said—a word that refers to an informal get-together, a time when rank and position are laid aside as much as possible and people who enjoy karate gather for a good time. Maybe that's why we rarely hear of gasshuku in this country: Perhaps here, where rank and title is a big deal, martial artists are more comfortable with seminars and their boot-camp mentality. Too bad.

Sleeping bags, campfire cooking and the inevitable 3 a.m. rainstorm are par for the course at gasshuku. So are budding friendships, fond memories and the camaraderie of shared hardship. As far as I know, no one has ever issued a certificate for attendance to a gasshuku. And because everyone is expected to participate in the training and in the chores, a lot of the big-name masters might not be around. But we could do with a few more gasshuku. I'll bring the watermelons; you blow up the balloons.

# TAKING CARE OF A VISITING TEACHER
*October 2002*

It was late. And hot. I'd been driving all day to get to the house where we were staying, and so had four other senior students. The juniors were all asleep in various rooms and out in the yard, and I wished to be among them. I was not, and neither were the other seniors, because the *sensei* was on his way. His plane was delayed, and it was nearly midnight before he touched down. When a sensei of his status arrives, the seniors have to be there to greet him. It isn't a rule written down anywhere, but it's part of *tetsudai*, an important element of *budo* training.

In the parlance of the Japanese arts, the word describes the duties of those who take care of a visiting teacher. There aren't a lot of arcane rituals to tetsudai. Most of the tasks are just common-sense courtesies you'd extend to any guest and being sensitive to the needs of the visiting teacher. Sensei—especially Japanese sensei or those influenced by Japanese culture—are sometimes reticent to express any needs, so you have to try to anticipate them. Does he have enough blankets in his room? Is he getting water during hot training sessions? Are we tiring him excessively, keeping him awake too late by asking all kinds of questions during post-training

> *Sensei*—especially Japanese sensei or those influenced by Japanese culture—are sometimes reticent to express any needs, so you have to try to anticipate them.

conversations? These are the sorts of questions the person responsible for tetsudai must ask and should answer as quickly as possible.

It's best when all the seniors take some responsibility for tetsudai because one may think of something that does not occur to another. The downside of this is that Bob can assume Bill has taken care of the visitor, while Bill assumes Bob has handled everything. "I thought *you* were waking him up this morning," is not what you want to hear at 6:30 a.m. on the first day of a training camp when a few dozen people are standing in a wet field, eager to get things going.

One of the saddest aspects of the budo as they've evolved in the West is the abuse of the practice of tetsudai by senior teachers. High-ranked instructors visit to give a clinic and expect to be placed in first-class hotels and taken to expensive restaurants, where they apparently think nothing of racking up substantial bills. The person responsible for tetsudai under these circumstances must grit his teeth and dole out the money for meeting these expenses, I suppose, but he should know this is not really in the spirit of the budo. It's just a case of an insensitive clod abusing his position.

Such abuse of tetsudai isn't confined to sensei from the martial arts. I know one *ikebana* teacher who starts fretting every June because she must do tetsudai for a Japanese flower-arranging sensei during his annual visits. He can, shall we say, put away the brew. She starts allocating funds to pay his bar tab at the beginning of every year. A tea ceremony teacher visiting this country a few years ago pushed tetsudai to the extreme when, after a long night of eating and drinking, he indicated that he would enjoy some professional companionship for the remainder of the evening and expected his host to procure it. The Japanese host was an old lady who was utterly horrified by the request, and she turned to her senior American students in desperation. It says a lot for those students that they stepped in and explained directly to the teacher that the services he had requested were illegal, immoral and inappropriate.

Of course, there are faults in the execution of tetsudai from the other side, as well. There is a well-known story of an *aikido* teacher who was asked to teach at a large convocation of aikido practitioners. It was a weeklong affair, and several sensei had been invited. Unfortunately, the organizers weren't particularly organized and didn't know much about tetsudai. When dinner was being served the first evening, either they assumed the teacher would show up or they just forgot about him. He ended up missing the meal. He called a taxi to go to the airport and left that night. His reasonable assumption was that, if the seniors had so little understanding of tetsudai that they didn't think to ensure an instructor was being fed, they probably weren't very serious about other aspects of their training.

A visiting sensei does not expect to be treated as if his stay is a license to plunder the resources and graciousness of his hosts. He is conscious that, in exchange for his teaching, the students are going to some trouble to make his stay comfortable and enjoyable, and he is grateful for this. True, he is doing them a favor by teaching them, and they are doing him a service by being good students and carrying on the art. But the hosts are not slaves who are available every moment to meet the sensei's every whim. Rather, they should be thoughtful, remain cognizant that an esteemed visitor is in their midst, and make reasonable efforts to ensure his stay is a good one. That is tetsudai.

# THE ART OF TEACHING
*January 2003*

From time to time, the responsibility has fallen on me to teach a *kata* to a junior in the *dojo*. "Teach" is probably the wrong word; I basically just introduce the outer movements to the student so he can begin to memorize their order—the first step in internalizing the form.

Teaching kata is extraordinarily difficult. Someone like me, who is not a qualified *sensei*, has no business doing it. I can show the movements and help the student memorize them, but only someone who is at a teaching level can properly transmit the heart of the kata. We who are not sensei—who are merely seniors in the dojo—occasionally find ourselves pressed into the job. When that happens, we need to remember how we were taught and try to do it the same way.

The biggest problem for most of us when we try to teach a kata—or anything from basic etiquette to individual techniques—is that we try to tell the student everything we have learned about it up to that very moment in too short a time. We forget that we were taught some of the subtler aspects of the form over a very long period. We certainly didn't get them all at once.

The tendency to "over-teach" is understandable. We have a natural impulse to want to give the junior the benefit of our experience. (We may

> The biggest problem for most of us when we try to teach a *kata*—or anything from basic etiquette to individual techniques—is that we try to tell the student everything we have learned about it up to that very moment in too short a time.

also enjoy showing off how much we know.) We want him to be able to grasp the kata from the perspective we have, but teaching this way, no matter how well-intended, is largely a waste of time. The student cannot possibly absorb everything in one session, and he will rapidly become confused and distracted, as evidenced by the glazing-over of his eyes and the faltering of his attention. If we try to cram in more information, he'll stop listening altogether as he tries to process what we've already given him. Amid the confusion, the student will often end up concentrating on the wrong elements of our instruction.

All kata of the Japanese arts are dependent on a Confucian-inspired methodology. Confucius, when he wasn't writing epigrams for fortune cookies, explained it best: Give a student one angle, and expect him to come up with the other three angles necessary to complete the square. In other words, the student must take the initiative in his martial arts education, at least to some degree. He has to study, think and observe—and see and appreciate connections that are not immediately obvious. For instance, a teacher may show him how to enhance a particular move in one form by doing this or that; he will not, however, explain that movements in other kata may be similarly improved. The student must see this relationship and apply it on his own.

This form of instruction is not common today. Students are accustomed to paying for lessons, and in return, they expect the teacher to work with them until they have learned the material. If they cannot grasp something, they take it for granted that the teacher will come up with another way to get the information across. This is not the traditional way of teaching. Martial artists who enter a traditional dojo expecting a modern instructional approach will quickly become very disappointed and frustrated.

As noted above, the average senior practitioner cannot correctly teach a kata and should not try. At best, he can demonstrate the movements for the purposes of allowing the junior student to watch and learn them in the correct order. For it to be anything more than a dance, however, the form must be taught over a long period by a qualified teacher. The form will slowly unfold before the student, partially through his own intense efforts. Teaching is a difficult job, and I'm reminded each time I try to do it how much I still have to learn.

# THE ESSENCE OF BUDO

*May 2003*

The inability of some Westerners to understand the essence of the *budo* has been a recurring topic in my columns. In fact, I've addressed the subject so often that readers might think I believe Westerners are a bunch of barbarians who could never appreciate the profound mysteries of the budo. This is not the case. America offers its citizens a greater potential for exploring other cultures than does any other country.

No, I don't have a quarrel with the West. I have, instead, a contention: It is sometimes extremely difficult to understand certain aspects of other cultures, and the misunderstandings that arise often have unexpected and undesirable consequences. This happens when Westerners try to thoroughly learn something from the East and when Easterners try to master something from the West.

Consider the following Japanese quotes: "There are a lot of people who practice faithfully, but I wonder if they really have a feel for it," and, "It's impressive superficially, but it's actually still quite shallow." Although they may sound like statements about Western *karateka*, they were actually made about Japanese musicians performing Western music.

Music in Japan does not consist of only *taiko* drumming and bamboo flute tunes. Western classical music is very popular there. Ten professional

---

## We are not doomed, by virtue of our birthplace, never to "get" the real stuff, never to penetrate the depths of understanding.

---

symphonies exist in Tokyo alone, and every high school has a classical orchestra. Brahms, Beethoven and Bach are as well-known to the Japanese as any native composer—and not just among the adult audiences that classical music mostly attracts in the United States. It might seem as if Western classical music has been completely assimilated into Japanese culture. Look more closely, though, and you'll get a different perspective.

Several Japanese critics note that for many Japanese—especially the younger ones—concerts are more about socializing than appreciating music. They also complain that Japanese performers are mechanical; their music, though technically correct, never shows any individuality.

"The principal defect of Japanese performers," one critic said, "is that they never seem to have strong opinions about the music they play." Takashi

Funayama, a music professor at Tokyo University of Arts, compared classical music in Japan to a blossom floating on a pond: "It's big and very beautiful, but it has no roots."

Many of the same criticisms are made about the budo in the West. A lot of non-Japanese *budoka* are vocal in their assertions that the martial arts transcend culture. They dismiss the native culture as, at best, a superfluity. They are correct: The movements, lessons and spiritual path provided by the budo are open to anyone who is sincere and dedicated. They are wrong, however, in asserting that the attendant culture of the martial arts has no weight.

The Westerner who was raised in a civilization dyed in the hues of Christianity has a different feel for music that was inspired and composed within the paradigms of that civilization. A familiarity with that religion and a lifelong conversance with that culture provide an insight and perspective on the music that are very difficult for one not similarly equipped.

Does that mean an ensemble in Keokuk, Iowa, will automatically perform Bach's Minuet in G major better than one in Kyoto? No. It means that the folks in Keokuk will have a perception and a shared understanding of aspects of the music that are difficult for a non-Westerner to grasp. It is ignorant to believe race or place of birth somehow conveys a special privileged power for understanding aspects of culture. Conversely, it is arrogant to believe each of us is automatically equal in approaching the world's different cultures.

That is one of the challenges we face in trying to master the budo, but the obstacles we encounter in overcoming our unfamiliarity with Japanese culture are not insurmountable. We are not doomed, by virtue of our birthplace, never to "get" the real stuff, never to penetrate the depths of understanding. We must acknowledge, though, that the budo have been fostered in a culture that is very different from our own and that the influences of that culture have not been incidental. We must understand that we don't come to the *dojo* with a cultural decoder.

It's a daunting task—and arguably more formidable than the one faced by Japanese musicians trying to get to the heart of Bach. The question is, Are you up to it?

# THE RIGHT AMOUNT OF VIOLENCE

*June 2003*

I saw something that was rumored to be an *aikido* demonstration the other day. After issuing a rambling explanation of the mysterious forces that gave the practitioners their powers, the teacher held the microphone with one hand and threw his students with the other. In another demo, a student threw an open-hand strike at a classmate's forehead, but because the defender was flustered, he allowed the force of the strike to peter out, and they both giggled. Later, the teacher faced another student. Both were armed with *bokken*, but their exchanges were so feeble that the wooden weapons barely clicked when they connected.

The saddest part was that the teacher and students seemed to believe they were doing a good job. No doubt they'd been taught that this was a legitimate expression of the Japanese *budo*. In their introduction, they mentioned kindness, etiquette and perseverance, all hallmarks of the budo and probably goals in their lives. Unfortunately, they'll never reach those goals, at least not the way they were practicing their art. They had no sense of *nangyo*—the impetus of hardship—which is sometimes translated as violence.

---

**From training outside in severe weather to testing for rank, the *budo* are full of hardships that act as a sculptor's tools to chisel away the extraneous and create the character of the mature *budoka*.**

---

Just as excessively macho approaches to the martial way are dangerously biased toward the physical, some arts weigh too heavily on their intellectual or spiritual properties. To understand why some violence is necessary in the budo, it helps to know a couple of terms that come from Buddhism.

*Tariki* and *jiriki* refer to ways in which the faithful can attain salvation. In some forms of Buddhism, salvation comes through some miraculous event. This is tariki. In other forms, it comes through hard work. This is jiriki, enlightenment through effort, or "the hard way."

The budo have numerous examples of tariki and jiriki. Ittosai Kagehisa, founder of the *itto ryu* of swordsmanship, secluded himself at a shrine in Kamakura, Japan, and trained day and night. He starved himself and constantly prayed for divine intervention to learn the essence of the sword. On the last evening of his stay, he was attacked from behind while training.

Ittosai whirled, deflecting the blade and killing the assailant in one stroke. He attributed the cut to the deities of the shrine and formed a school around the technique.

Another example involves aikido founder Morihei Uyeshiba. A Japanese army *kendo* instructor challenged the young Uyeshiba to a friendly contest. It got out of hand, and the instructor supposedly went full force with his sword, trying to hit his unarmed opponent. After successfully avoiding the attacks, Uyeshiba claimed that he received a divine message about the true meaning of his art.

While both stories have an air of tariki about them, remember that they occurred *after* Ittosai and Uyeshiba had spent years training hard. One of the humorous messages in Eiji Yoshikawa's book about the life of Miyamoto Musashi tells how the young swordsman constantly searched for some mystical secret of mastery, not knowing that the real secrets don't come from the gods but through daily training. The principles of the budo can't be mastered through transcendent illumination. They are not tariki. They are jiriki, and so the path to their perfection is one of *nangyo-do*, the way of hardship.

From training outside in severe weather to testing for rank, the budo are full of hardships that act as a sculptor's tools to chisel away the extraneous and create the character of the mature *budoka*. But it's the most elemental of struggles, that of grappling with another person during a conflict, which produces an essential facet of that character. Your spirit is solidified by the threat of danger, the possibility of injury or death, and knowing that you may inflict that fate on another person. While difficult and sometimes painful and frightening, no amount of philosophical pondering can take the place of these confrontations if you are ever to grasp the meaning of the budo.

Does that mean training in the martial ways is an endless bloodbath? No. It means that, just as every form of the Japanese ways helps refine character, so do the budo. In *chado*, the way of tea, character is molded by the aesthetic appreciation of beauty and form and by the sometimes boring, sometimes challenging process of making tea under all sorts of circumstances. In the budo, character is built in part through violence and struggle. Without them, judo, *karate-do* and the like are no longer "martial," and while they may be "ways" of some kind, they cannot be construed as martial ways.

I am not suggesting that your training is inadequate unless your *dojo* is strewn with broken bodies. However, sprains, bloody noses, cut lips and other minor injuries are part of the journey.

One question remains: If violence is an accepted and expected part of training, how can you know whether your dojo is really a place for learning the way or simply a glorified boxing gym? In other words, what's the difference between a real dojo and a place that allows bullies and sadists to run free? The difference lies in the word nangyo. *Nan* is written with a character that means "extremely difficult" or "bordering on the impossible." *Gyo* refers to a "stage" in the training process. It comes from a character that translates literally as "crossroads where many people come and go." Gyo implies a step along the way, a process of becoming or going somewhere, and not a state of completion or a destination. In the budo, violence isn't an end in itself. It isn't a goal worth pursuing for its own sake. It's a path to a higher stage. With this in mind, you should be able to observe the activity at a traditional dojo and make the distinction easily.

Many boxers, professional wrestlers and full-contact fighters employ violence regularly in their lives. But whatever their goals, they aren't budoka. While we share a link with them because we are involved in fighting, our intents are markedly different. For us, nangyo-do is part of a journey leading to something far beyond money or self-satisfaction. Jigoro Kano described it well: "By training you in attacks and defenses, it refines your body and your soul and helps you make the spiritual essence of judo a part of your very being. In this way, you are able to perfect yourself and create something of value to the world."

# POSTURING

*July 2003*

Life today imposes tremendous pressure on teenagers and perhaps even more on adolescent boys. They're supposed to act mature and look grown-up to attain the status, or at least the appearance, of adulthood. They often can't, however, so they posture. Watch teenagers where they congregate, and you'll see their gestures are so contrived that they make runway models look natural.

I mention this because the temptations and opportunities to posture are just as overwhelming in the *budo*. Years ago, an acquaintance told me his friend had asked to be shown a karate stance that would make him look like he knew what he was doing. That person didn't actually want to train in karate; he just wanted to look like he had.

By posturing, I'm not talking about *kamae* (stances assumed during training) necessarily, although in some ways, these can be a kind of posturing, as well. My nomination for the most embarrassing stance in martial arts history goes to Danny LaRusso in *The Karate Kid*, hopping around on one leg, arms flapping like a jackass. I guess the producers thought the spectacle would look "karate-esque." But as I said, I'm not talking about stances per se; I'm talking about the affectations and mannerisms that are

---

**My nomination for the most embarrassing stance in martial arts history goes to Danny LaRusso in *The Karate Kid*, hopping around on one leg, arms flapping like a jackass.**

---

designed and adopted to give a person a sense of power or status, if only in his own mind.

Swaggering is a classic kind of martial arts posturing, most often seen in the "fat master waddle"—the unmistakable gait of the overweight, middle-aged martial artist. He attempts to strut, but his belly gets in the way and turns it into a waddle, with his shoulders rowing back and forth like pistons. It is an affectation, a posture that's supposed to convey the notion that "I am somebody"—as if the red-and-white striped belt with 20 hash marks aren't enough.

Flicking out punches or kicks while playing around with the guys, wearing your uniform to a burger joint because you didn't feel like changing after practice, meditating in the park, and showing off your "numchuck skills" are all forms of posturing. Those who engage in these activities try to give the impression that they're just behaving normally, but they're obviously trying to draw attention.

It just looks silly, and it has exactly the opposite effect of what was intended. The best example I've seen of this is in Hawaii. There are four agencies near Waikiki where you can rent a red Ferrari like the one on *Magnum, P.I.* Now, what kind of logic runs through the mind of the guy who rents one of these? Does he think girls will be attracted to him? Is he going to fight crime? The charade is far more pathetic than cool. The same goes for the martial artist.

Maybe the most important argument against posturing for the *karateka* is that doing so relies heavily on illusion, while karate should focus on truth. Karate is a constant struggle. The struggle is physical, but it's also psychological and emotional. Let the bald guy comb those few strands of hair over his dome to fool himself and others into believing he's still got a full head of hair. Allow the grandmother to wear miniskirts and outlandish makeup to convince everyone she's still a hot babe. That kind of superficial nonsense is for people who can't or won't see the truth about themselves; it is not for the karateka.

Remember what your *sensei* has probably told you again and again: Karate is natural. The movements are simple and unaffected. At some point in your training, it should strike you that the naturalness of the art extends beyond the physical techniques, and acting natural in your daily life is the clearest indication that you are absorbing the lessons of the way.

## TEACHERS AND STUDENTS
*October 2003*

How many students does a good teacher have? How many *should* he have? Is there a limit to the number of students one person can legitimately and competently instruct?

Some training halls boast that they have hundreds of students, while others insist they have even more. A few schools even use the number of students they claim to have in their advertising. I guess it works for them, but I'm not sure I'd be all that excited about consulting a doctor or lawyer who advertises that people were waiting in lines around the block to get in. I'd be afraid I wouldn't receive any individualized attention or personal service. But people might go to those martial arts training halls for different reasons.

An *aikido* teacher I know once said that not all who trained with him were his students. I think he meant that just paying the fees and attending classes did not guarantee the student his serious consideration. That, he explained, is how things were done in the "old days."

It's certainly possible to understand that teacher's perspective: Pay your tuition and you have access to the *dojo* and to some kind of instruction. Stay long enough and show initiative and drive, and eventually the *sensei* will

---

**Even if we accept that not all who train under the direction of a *sensei* are specifically his students, the question remains, How many pupils can a teacher have and still be effective?**

---

begin to notice you. Stay even longer, and he'll consider you his student. Fair enough. But if I were to take that path, I hope I'd be honest enough to tell prospective students about my point of view upfront.

Even if we accept that not all who train under the direction of a sensei are specifically his students, the question remains, How many pupils can a teacher have and still be effective?

I once met the senior student of a well-known karate teacher in the United States. The student started training with his master soon after he arrived from Japan 20 years earlier. Of the thousands of students who'd come and gone, he was among the few that had stuck it out. Making conversation, I asked what kind of home his sensei lived in. "I don't know," the student said. "I've never been there."

He was surprised at my surprise. I wanted to ask, "How could you spend two decades in a relationship as close as the one between a teacher and student and never have been in the guy's house?" The fellow said he'd met his teacher's wife once and seen his children a few times. That was the scope of his interaction with his sensei outside the dojo. Perhaps I'm naive, but I wonder how much any man could influence me if, in 20 years together, the occasion to get to know his spouse and children had never arisen.

Was this man a student of the sensei? Indisputably, in some ways. In some respects, every person who comes in contact with a teacher for the sake of instruction is a student of that teacher. Sometimes a teacher will do or say something during a momentary exchange that he will have forgotten five minutes later, but it will have a profound effect on the student for years to come. It's possible, too, to teach a student for 20 years and never have any significant influence on him. This should also have some resonance in a wide range of matters, including your motivation in seeking a teacher and your motivation to teach.

In the end, the answer to my initial question may be that the teacher might never know how many students he has—or how few.

# FORGING AHEAD
*November 2003*

Some years ago, I interviewed the author of a best-selling book on stretching and conditioning. He told me about a group of railroad workers in need of better physical fitness. Virtually every one of them, he said, was in terrible shape—extremely overweight and inflexible. Their work on the railroad was physically demanding, but once they got home, they just sat in front of the television and ate potato chips.

What was unusual about this group, the author said, was that nearly all of them had been active in high-school athletics. Most had played football or basketball at the varsity level, and the majority had been on championship teams. Now in their mid-30s, they were slugs. What happened?

The author explained that, during high school, physical training had consumed a considerable part of their day, but when the men joined the work force, opportunities to exercise virtually disappeared. "There was nothing in between for them," he told me. "Their engines were either in overdrive, like they were in high school, or they were idling, like they were when I met them."

Unfortunately, this approach to fitness is common. Physical activity is still seen by a lot of people as a pursuit for children. "I ran into an old high-school friend who'd started practicing karate when I did," a friend

---

**One's age, family, personal responsibilities and career place great demands on adults, but that doesn't mean we have to forfeit our training.**

---

told me recently. "When he found out I was still practicing 30 years later, he said, 'I can't believe you're still into that foolishness. You're too old for that!'" A similar attitude is seen in *budo* training: Too many people believe that, if they can't practice full-bore, they shouldn't practice at all.

This condition is predominant in Japanese karate, and I think I know why. In Japan, high school is a massive grind. Long hours are spent studying, and there's little time for anything else. But if your grades are good, you can get into a good university, and at that point you can coast—educationally speaking. College is seen as a time for slacking off and having fun before adulthood begins. Courses are relatively easy, and many college students in Japan spend more time participating in club activities than they do studying. It isn't unusual for members of university karate clubs to train five or six hours a day. This gung-ho, let's-punch-the-*makiwara*-until-our-knuckles-bleed approach can turn people into phenomenally good practitioners. Not coincidentally, it was such men who introduced karate to the rest of the world in the late 1950s and early '60s. They came to the United States and Europe, fresh from having trained almost as much as they slept, and they brought that attitude with them.

Besides those university students and the fanatical foreigners who come to Japan to train, almost nobody in Japan practices every day. For most Japanese, the train ride to the *dojo* is simply too much. Once they are out of school and working full time, they have to cut back on their training. Sometimes, they will make the same mistake as the railroad workers: "If I can't do it at an intense, nearly full-time level, I'm not going to do it at all."

Therein lies the problem. One's age, family, personal responsibilities and career place great demands on adults, but that doesn't mean we have to forfeit our training. We must learn to go from overdrive to a more relaxed gear while still forging ahead.

Sadly, too many instructors try to perpetuate those artificial expectations of training. I have heard of teachers who tell their students that skipping a single class will reduce their reaction time. Such a drop in performance—perhaps measurable only under laboratory conditions—may have some effect if they are competing at an international level, but it is doubtful that a 45-year-old second-degree black belt will notice a significant dip in his progress because he wasn't able to train last Thursday.

It is a mistake to believe that budo training will have no value if you cannot practice several hours a day like you did when you were single, childless, unemployed or otherwise free to train. You must learn to maximize the hours you do spend in the dojo. The time you have for budo is not fixed, and you may have to cut back occasionally, but as long as you continue training, you'll enjoy the benefits your art has to offer.

# THE HARMONY OF THE TONFA

*December 2003*

"For me, the *tonfa* is a symbol of harmony," Kina-*san* once told me. A friend of my karate teacher's, Kina-san used to give some impressive demonstrations with a pair of his favorite weapons. I had seen him spin a tonfa and catch a solid wooden staff that was being swung at him, then hit it with such force that the staff cracked. So I had my doubts about the harmony stuff.

The simple tonfa, originally a handle used to rotate a gristmill, is often overshadowed by flashier Okinawan weapons, but it is every bit as effective and deadly as any other component of the makeshift armament of the *Ryukyu*. I had been shown graphically how it could generate enough force to smash bones and pulverize organs. I couldn't begin to guess how it could possibly symbolize harmony.

Kina-san was born in Hawaii, but he spent his high-school years living with relatives in Okinawa. He trained extensively in karate there. He returned to Hawaii in 1940, just before the bombing of Pearl Harbor. It was bad timing. Fearing imprisonment at the hands of U.S. authorities, he spent most of the next four years living in a friend's hunting cabin in a rural part of Maui, gardening to feed himself and practicing with the tonfa to pass the time.

One summer evening, I asked Kina-san what he had meant when he said the tonfa was a symbol of harmony. He explained that, while appearing to be of simple construction, the tonfa is actually a complicated tool to build. It must be fashioned carefully to withstand the tremendous stress of combat and the abuse of daily training. The Okinawans discovered that a long time ago when they began adapting various farming and fishing tools for combat.

Regionally called a tonfa, *tunfa* or *tuifa*, it was originally made from a native species of tree similar to our white oak. These tonfa—the word means "handle"—were used on millstones. The projecting knob was inserted into a hole in the mill's upper stone, and the longer shaft was used as a handle to rotate it against the lower stone. Used this way, relatively little stress was placed on the tonfa. When they were adapted as weapons, though, the Okinawans discovered the tonfa often broke where the knob was inserted into the shaft. Several experiments failed to produce a tonfa that could hold up during combat.

Eventually—and I hasten to add that Kina-san admitted this was a folk

tale, possibly true but not to be considered history—a farmer noticed that fishing boats were patched with wooden plugs similar in circumference to the knob of a tonfa. The plugs, called *fundu*, were subject to similar stresses. If the fishermen could craft a plug that was watertight and still flexible enough to withstand the motion of the boat, he reasoned, the same technology could be applied to the tonfa.

The flaw in his plan was that a rivalry existed between many farming and fishing communities in Okinawa. People who lived only a mile away were considered outsiders, and few would have dreamed of approaching them to ask a favor. Yet that is exactly what the farmers decided to do.

Two of them volunteered to go to the fishing community and humbled themselves by asking for advice about making the tonfa stronger. They learned that the method of wood joinery was known only to a couple of local fishing families. The farmers went to them and were surprised to be met with respect.

The fishermen took the farmers down to the beach and shared their knowledge. One secret of the fundu was that they used a part of the *iju*, a tropical tree indigenous to Okinawa that has been employed in the making of seagoing canoes and boats for centuries. Sections of iju wood were cut across the grain and then soaked in seawater to make them fit tightly while remaining flexible.

The farmers thanked their unexpected benefactors for revealing the method. Then one of them asked, "Why did you share your secrets with us when there has always been so much distance between farmers and fishermen?" Members of the two fishing families explained that, several generations ago, the fishermen needed a wood that was supple and strong to repair their boats. Frustrated by their lack of success in locating anything suitable, one of them had finally gone to a nearby community and sought out a farmer who was famous for his woodworking skills. It was that man who taught them to use the iju wood for their plugs. By instructing the two farmers, the fishermen said, they were in a sense repaying a favor once done for their ancestors.

Whether it is a true story is a matter of conjecture; one frequently hears these sorts of tales about the old days in Okinawa. Even so, I have compared some older versions of tonfa made by expert craftsmen with modern factory-produced units. With knobs that are pegged or glued, the newer models will hold up for a while, but sooner or later, they'll crack or loosen. The old ones, however, stay strong and tight no matter how hard they're used. It makes me wonder whether there isn't some truth to Kina-san's story.

# HARDBODIES

*February 2004*

"I've got to get stronger." So said Ben, a former training partner who was close to 60. He'd always been careful about his diet and got regular exercise in addition to his *budo* training, but then something happened. Perhaps he simply woke up one morning and realized he was no longer in his 30s, when a hard workout would mean a day or two of recovery and we'd be ready to go again. Now it took twice that long. Now there were the aches, pains and stiff joints we never had before. We didn't bounce back the way we used to.

If it hasn't happened to you yet, you'll see it by the time you reach middle age, when your sense of mortality sneaks up and taps you on the shoulder. When it does, you'll probably react in one of several ways.

Ben chose to meet the limitations of age by charging at it head-on. He began a program of weightlifting. In addition to the popular magazines about muscular development, his reading material included obscure journals devoted to increasing strength and muscle mass. He was constantly holding a grip exerciser. He bought all sorts of mineral supplements and powders to make his body stronger. Clearly, he was trying to fortify his physical self. He was shoring up the castle defenses, making the walls

---

**The simple truth is that, no matter how we try to harden ourselves against the world's threats, either in a physical or emotional sense, we cannot succeed entirely and still be alive.**

---

thicker and taller. Old age might come to others, but not to him. He was going to make himself so strong that he could stave off illness as well as any other depredations time had in store for him.

Training regularly with Ben, I soon noticed a difference—his grip became markedly more powerful, for instance. But I also noticed something else: The quality of it had changed. When he grabbed my wrist, his fingers and palm felt almost brittle, like someone had wrapped a plaster cast around my arm. When I shifted my body to effect a pin or throw, he could maintain his grip for only a short time. There was no flexibility in his hold, and when it reached the end of the short range of motion it had, the power dwindled.

As soon as you grab someone who's trained in *aikido, jujutsu* or any of the grappling arts, you must be instantly receptive to his movement if you want to control him. You don't grab so much as you palpate his wrist. Then, when he tries to escape or turn the attack against you, you can shift and prevent it. Ben had lost his ability to do that.

Of course, the myth of becoming muscle-bound is just that: a myth. Proper weight training always includes a lot of stretching and other supplemental exercises, and it's a perfectly reasonable way to increase strength. Physiologists report that it can be beneficial for people in their 70s and beyond. In Ben's case, however, I don't think it was his strength that he wanted to improve. A lifetime of exercise and many years of budo training had made him very strong and fit. He wanted to be *harder*—and that's an entirely different proposition.

After the introduction of firearms in Japan, castle construction changed dramatically. Walls became higher and thicker, and the structures assumed truly formidable dimensions. They were so effective at the end of the age of the samurai that they were rarely successfully breached by combat or siege; they were usually taken because of what happened not outside the walls but within. A castle defender—for pay or some other motivation—would unlock a gate or lower a ladder, allowing the enemy to enter. Consequently, those living behind the walls couldn't rely on the castle's outer strength alone but had to be sensitive to what was going on inside, as well.

Therein lies a lesson that relates to the path Ben took to defend against the onslaught of age. The simple truth is that, no matter how we try to harden ourselves against the world's threats, either in a physical or emotional sense, we cannot succeed entirely and still be alive. Illness and disease will find a way in, and in some cases might actually spawn from within us. If we have a heart, it's going to be broken or at least banged around a few times in our lives. Being strong is always good, but being flexible is even better.

I've trained with a lot of older *budoka* who have attained a high degree of skill. In a test of raw strength, I probably could have beaten most of them at arm-wrestling or weightlifting. I was never impressed with how strong they were, but I was impressed with the way they moved. They were relaxed. They wasted no motion in initiating action, and there wasn't any warm-up or preparation. They went from point A to point D, and I never saw points B or C at all.

When responding to an attack, they seemed to be suspended in time until the last possible fraction of a second, when they were out of range of the attack and their counter was completed. They never seemed to be rigid

or inflexible. The power was always there, and it appeared instantaneously and at just the right time, then it was invisible again, and they were loose and fluid once more.

Most of you probably weren't born when Simon and Garfunkel were big, and you might have never heard their hit song "I Am a Rock." It was popular with young people because it expressed the attitude of shutting oneself off from love and the potential trouble it creates. "I am a rock, I am an island," was one line; "A rock feels no pain," was another. This sentiment is consistent with the martial arts philosophy *iwao no mi*, which is Japanese for "body of a rock." Physically and emotionally, we must turn ourselves to stone, it says.

That approach didn't work with Ben. He dropped out of the budo. He also, I heard not long after, dropped out of a relationship that failed. He made his body harder—and maybe his spirit, as well. He lost the flexibility to relate to the motion and intentions of his training partners. He lost the flexibility to relate to others around him, too.

If Ben had really wanted to be stronger, I would have agreed with him. I want to be stronger, as well, and I work to achieve that goal. But I don't think my body or spirit needs to be any harder. And I don't think a harder spirit will take me where I want to go in my training. Or anywhere else.

# MARTIAL ARTS ETIQUETTE

*March 2004*

Those of us who lived through the turbulence of the 1960s remember the battering taken by cultural conventions like courtesy and formality. In that era of "do your own thing," manners became a symbol of discipline and were thought to be oppressive and contrary to creativity.

Despite the changes that were affecting society at the time, *budo* instructors insisted that their students conform to traditional Japanese courtesies. While many of them supported their students' idealistic search for freedom, they didn't budge in demanding those students observe the strict conventions of *reishiki*, or etiquette. And so it is today.

In the West, we have an adage: Manners are nothing more than a series of minor inconveniences undertaken to make life more pleasant for others. In much the same spirit, the samurai developed an elaborate system of deportment that made his world a more comfortable, predictable place. This, again, is reishiki.

Some of the samurai's courtesies were shared by the rest of Japanese society. For example, when *tatami* mats became popular in urban areas, removing shoes at the door became common. And because Japan's highways were vulnerable to robbers and brigands, men adopted the habit of walking a couple of paces ahead of the women in their company. Over

---

**If you observe the spirit of *reishiki* as a part of your daily life and make it an unconscious component of your interactions with others, in an emergency you'll react with the same kind of spontaneity.**

---

the years, that protective measure evolved into a courtesy that has only recently begun to disappear.

Other manners of reishiki applied specifically to the samurai. When a commoner visited someone at home or saw an acquaintance on the street, he used any one of about a dozen greetings. For the samurai, however, the formal greeting was *gomen nasai* ("I'm sorry," or "Pardon me"), which represented an apology for intruding on the thoughts or affairs of another.

Perhaps the best-known practice of samurai reishiki pertained to the care and handling of swords that were being examined or held by men other than their owners. When passing a sword to another person, for instance, one had to be sure the weapon's hand guard was toward the left with the blade's edge away from the receiver. The person receiving it had to grip the hilt with his left hand and remove the blade from its sheath in a way that didn't appear combative.

Often, the rigidity for manners proves difficult for later generations to understand. In his book *Something Like an Autobiography*, the late film director Akira Kurosawa recalls an incident during his childhood when a pot of oil caught fire in his family's house. Grabbing the blazing container in her bare hands, his mother raced out to the garden before the oil could spill and ignite the whole kitchen. It wouldn't have done for a polite person to walk in the garden barefoot, however, so with the pot blistering her hands, she paused at the doorway to put on wooden clogs.

A less dramatic display of etiquette is recounted in Gichin Funakoshi's autobiography, *Karate-do: My Way of Life*. He had just come to Japan from Okinawa and took a job as a janitor in a Tokyo University dormitory. Whenever a visitor would inquire about receiving karate training from Funakoshi, he would excuse himself, rush up to his room and change into a formal *kimono* before answering.

It would have been more practical for Kurosawa's mother and Funakoshi to dispense with manners in those situations, but they were products of the Meiji Era in Japan, the last age of feudalism on earth, and propriety was as important to them as life itself.

The modern *budoka* doesn't have to contend with nearly as much reishiki. Indeed, today's practitioner is merely expected to bow at the right time and sit in the correct manner. However, these elementary formalities are unnecessary in learning an art like karate, so why do *sensei* demand them?

The reason for reishiki in the *dojo* is twofold. First, it's a basic tenet of the budo that the way to live honestly, respectfully and free from distractions is to immerse yourself regularly in an activity that suspends conscious thought. From that perspective, *how* you do something is at least as important as *what* you do. In disciplines like *iaido* and *kyudo*, practical application is virtually nonexistent. However, through reishiki, the devotee achieves a state of tranquillity that's very practical.

Second, manners make you more formidable in action. Funakoshi said, "Karate begins and ends with courtesy." He meant that you should be polite in and out of the dojo. If you observe the spirit of reishiki as a part of your daily life and make it an unconscious component of your interactions with others, in an emergency you'll react with the same kind of spontaneity.

The samurai writer Yamamoto Tsunetomo also expressed this in his book *Hagakure:* "Etiquette is to be quick at the beginning and end, and tranquil in the middle." One way of interpreting his words is to consider that, if the actions before a movement, *kata* or knife defense are natural and conform to reishiki, the better the chances are that the movement will be correct. That isn't to say you ought to pause and bow before kicking the snot out of an assailant. Rather, it means that if your breathing, timing and posture are maintained through reishiki, you're apt to find yourself more adaptable to unexpected or stressful situations.

Naturally, it wouldn't be worthwhile to spend years practicing something that might never be used. This brings us back to the reason why samurai considered reishiki to be important in their day and why manners are important to us now. By handing a sword to a companion with its cutting edge pointing away, the samurai assured his friend that he was looking out for his safety. By the simplest act, he made life more pleasant and comfortable. As martial artists whose heritage springs from a culture of warriors who placed so much emphasis on this kind of etiquette, we should remember that it's still an important part of our training.

# CLASSICAL RANK

*May 2004*

In the early years of martial arts, there was little need for rank. One person developed or acquired skills that were useful on the battlefield and passed them along to others, perhaps with little thought of a formal system. That's not to say there was no organized teaching. As early as the 12th century, discrete methods of combat were being taught. But it wasn't until the rise of the *ryu* in the 14th century that ranks had any value.

Ryu were, essentially, family businesses in which the founder of an art passed along his skills to the next generation. There wasn't anything like trademarks in Japan at that time, but ryu were considered the property of whoever developed or inherited them. As they became formal organizations, there was a need to acknowledge who was in and who was out, and where a person stood in the hierarchy of the school. There was a need to know who was officially granted permission to teach, and who had the ability to pass on the art completely and correctly. Consequently, nearly all ryu adopted a system of licensing.

*Menkyo* is the Japanese word for "license." In the classical martial arts, it almost always refers to a document giving one permission to teach or certifying that one has progressed to a particular level. The standards for granting menkyo are remarkably varied. In some ryu, there's only a single certification issued that recognizes your mastery of the system. In others,

---

**It's worthwhile to consider what the ramifications would have been if the *budo*, instead of adopting belt ranks, had continued with the *menkyo* system.**

---

many licenses are handed out—a progression not unlike the modern belt ranks. The initial license might indicate that you have been formally accepted into the ryu, while subsequent licenses might indicate your progress and denote permission to teach or otherwise represent it.

The names of menkyo can be misleading. For instance, the license of *oku-iri* means "entrance to the secrets," implying that it's an advanced certification. In fact, in the *shindo muso ryu* of *jojutsu*, it's the most basic one and merely signifies that you've entered into a formal relationship with the teacher. It's also possible to be granted the highest certification and still not have the necessary qualifications to teach formally. In these cases, permission is granted in some other way.

Most ryu grant some kind of certificate in the form of a document or scroll. A few, though, simply grant a verbal acknowledgment. If the menkyo is paper, the manner in which it's folded can be a sign of the level it indicates. They are most often called *kirigami*, or "cut paper." Scrolls, or *makimono*, are almost always used to confer advanced certifications. Sometimes they are laid out in the form of *mokuroku*, which list the techniques or *kata* of the ryu. Other makimono might contain the history of the ryu or references to patron deities or unique principles of the art.

It's the nature of a classical ryu that its innermost secrets are transmitted to very few people in any generation. This is also true of many flower-arrangement and tea-ceremony ryu, wherein the secrets are given only to a single inheritor who becomes the next headmaster in the lineage. (Sometimes a headmaster dies or becomes incapacitated before he can pass on this information. In this case, sadly, the ryu ceases to exist.)

In some cases, the mere possession of a full set of scrolls indicates the person has inherited the ryu. These are *sodensho*, or "records of inheritance." In others, the granting of a menkyo to confer succession of the system is signaled by *betsu-den no maki*, or "scrolls of special techniques." In some ryu, the headmaster or teacher writes each certificate out. In others, the student is presented with an earlier menkyo and expected to use it as a model to write his own license, which is then signed or sealed by his teacher. It's common now for menkyo to be professionally written by calligraphers. Consequently, some are works of art, and older ones are avidly collected in Japan by enthusiasts (who often can't begin to decipher what the document says).

The cost of a menkyo varies. In some ryu, there might be no charge. In others—and this is particularly true of flower arranging and tea ceremonies—the cost can be startling. The price can be in the four-figure range, especially if it indicates a right to teach.

It's worthwhile to consider what the ramifications would have been if the *budo*, instead of adopting belt ranks, had continued with the menkyo system. How would modern arts like karate be different under such a system? Would the ranks have more integrity? Would certain personalities be attracted to menkyo rather than the ladder-like progression of belt ranks? Would it be good for the martial arts? It's interesting to ponder.

# PREARRANGED SPARRING

*July 2004*

**M**any of you probably have never practiced prearranged sparring. Some *dojo* have eliminated it from their regular training; others have never included it in the first place. Some students find it boring—an unchallenging, static exercise that looks robotic and divorced from any kind of combative relevance. It might seem that way, but it isn't.

It's tough to describe prearranged sparring without illustrations. Think of it like this: You and I face each other in a front stance, each with our left leg out front. Stepping forward a full pace into a right front stance, I punch at your face. You step back with your left leg and block with your right fist. I step forward again and attack, this time on the left side. You step back and receive it again on your left side, blocking. I continue, stepping forward on the right side once more. You receive and slide forward and counter with a right reverse punch.

It sounds, as I said, like a boring way to train—especially because we have agreed what my attack and your counter will be. Prearranged sparring seems like the embodiment of the criticism often leveled at traditional karate. What do you do in "real life" if the attacker strikes other than where you've agreed? How many times does a real attacker launch three strikes in a straight line, one right after the other? In response to these questions, it's usually best to say, "Gee, I never thought of that, and neither did all those generations of *karateka* who came before me. We must really be dumb. Thanks for setting me straight."

Then go practice prearranged sparring. And learn.

Choreographed sequences of three-step sparring can vary. Instead of three steps, there can be four, five or just one. Collectively, they are called *yakusoku kumite*. Yakusoku means "agreement," in that we agree beforehand which attacks will be made. Despite the apparently artificial training environment it creates, yakusoku kumite is a fine way to hone your timing.

Let's repeat the sequence I just described. I make three punches, stepping forward right-left-right; you step back, blocking three times, and then counter. But this time, instead of stepping back on my third step, you slide forward as I make my final step, coming in at an angle to forestall my punch. Instead of blocking, you hit my midsection with a short vertical punch and break the rhythm I've established. This is the "stop-attack." Now we've moved into an entirely new area. You know where my final attack is going, so you don't have to worry about getting hit and can experiment with your counter. When is the best moment to slide in and interrupt my attack with one of your own? Is it as I begin to step forward or just as I'm about to finish? How can you generate maximum power over a shorter distance?

Sure, you could try the same kind of stop-attack in free-sparring, but you wouldn't be able to do it over and over again, to polish and refine it, because I wouldn't attack the same way repeatedly. You'd also be reluctant to move into the attack—a fundamental necessity for perfecting this kind of timing—if you were worried about which attack I might make. Prearranged kumite creates a laboratory in which you can experiment safely.

You can also play around with the angles of your counterattack. What vector offers the most targets or the best chance of getting in? How about stepping off to the side and countering with a roundhouse kick? You can also try shifting slightly offline to make a stop-attack front kick or some other counter.

Here's another training variation: I take the first two steps forward, punching each time—right leg forward, right punch, left leg, left punch—but instead of making the last attack a punch, I shift my weight back and do a left front-leg kick. You have to deal with the sudden change in distancing, receive the kick with your block and execute a counter. At this point, you can study the options of moving to the left or right of my kick. Is it easier to shift one way or another? Which side offers the best targets?

Now, let's return to the original three-step sequence. I end with a right punch, right leg forward. You have stepped back, first with your left leg and then with your right in response to the first two attacks. Instead of taking a full step back, however, you step back so your left foot is even with your right. Now you shift your weight, and in response to my final right-side punch, intercept my movement with a right-leg roundhouse kick.

In free-sparring, we tend to have optimal balance with our legs apart. Unfortunately, in a real fight or even in a tournament bout, that isn't always possible. In the controlled environment of prearranged sparring, you can see what happens when you can't kick from a balanced posture. Additionally, there are few better methods for building strong hip muscles. Prearranged sparring affords you an opportunity to have a moving target, and you can feel your hips deliver the power.

Once you've tried this kind of back-and-forth sequencing, you can add more steps. The variations are endless. The more complex they become, the more challenging they are. It's like trying to remember a *kata*, only in this case your imaginary opponent isn't imaginary, and if you make a mistake, you feel the consequences.

# ONE PUNCH, ONE KILL

*September 2004*

One of the more enduring legends of karate is the ability of an expert to kill with a single punch. The famous names of karate history, from Sokon Matsumura and Kyan Chotoku to many well-known teachers today, supposedly have settled encounters using a single, lethal blow. The power to extinguish a human life with one strike apparently not being enough for him, Masutatsu Oyama supposedly once used the technique against an unfortunate bull.

Karate legends, of course, are called that for a reason. Often there's little, if any, documentation of the feat, and original sources frequently prove more elusive than the Loch Ness monster. Modern tales about *karateka* who have allegedly killed with one punch tend to begin with, "Well, nobody wants to bring it up because my *sensei* doesn't like to talk about it, but one time he got cornered..."

At any rate, we have the legend of the one-punch kill, so what are we to make of it? Is it completely false? I doubt it. I recently read a newspaper article about a man who was sentenced to prison after a street fight. He hit his opponent just once, and the guy fell down, cracked his head on the sidewalk and died. We all know of tragic accidents in the boxing ring where a punch caused a cerebral hemorrhage or other injury, killing the boxer.

Sure, you say, but that's not what we're talking about. By a one-punch kill, we mean a strike so powerful and focused it causes the opponent to be definitively taken out. We want to know whether a karate technique has this fearsome power.

The Japanese expression for it is *ikken hisatsu*, which means "one-fist kill" or "one-punch kill." Originally, it meant "one-sword kill," with the character for "sword" being *ken*. However, written another way but pronounced the same, the word can mean "fist." The ability to take life with a single sword strike is certainly not difficult to imagine. One barely needs to nick an artery, and the blood loss could lead to death in a matter of minutes.

Ikken hisatsu was a combative reality on the samurai's battlefield and in the duels fought during the latter stages of Japan's feudal period, when swordsmen were unarmored. But when did it become part of karate's ancient lore?

It's worthwhile to note that there are very few mentions of it in Okinawan sources. In Choki Motobu's *Okinawa Kempo*, the author writes, "Deaths have occurred ... in karate matches ... even by one strike," but he includes no specifics. Such vague references tend to be common; the literature surrounding

Okinawan karate is scant and sometimes unreliable. If we look at oral legends and anecdotes, we still find no substantiation of this amazing ability.

I suspect that ikken hisatsu became a part of karate history when the art was brought to mainland Japan early in the 20th century. Eager to have it accepted as a legitimate *budo* form, leaders like Gichin Funakoshi adopted Japanese names for *kata* and initiated the practice of wearing uniforms similar to those of judo. It seems understandable that they would copy some of the concepts of budo, as well. If the idea of killing with a single sword cut was part of the philosophy of the traditional Japanese warrior, they might have thought, Why not link it to karate?

If we accept my theory that ikken hisatsu is little more than an attempt to make karate seem more traditionally Japanese, we might conclude that the motives of those involved were a bit tacky. In the same vein, today we see certain combative arts suddenly stressing weapons, animal forms and meditative practices because they've recently become popular and "hip."

Perhaps there's something to that conclusion, but I think we're selling short karate's early pioneers in Japan. They may have attached ikken hisatsu to their art to make it seem more Japanese, but they also used the expression to make a good point. For most of us, killing a person with one punch is unlikely. No matter how powerful we are, what speed we have or what technical accuracy we can generate, human beings are fairly resilient, especially when they're fighting back, moving and otherwise ruining our efforts to attack them.

What's important about ikken hisatsu is the mentality it represents. Certainly you might not kill with a single punch, but if we're going to fight, you must attack me exactly in that spirit. You must go into the encounter believing that a single strike will decide it all. Funakoshi once noted that we must regard our opponent's limbs as if they were knives and swords. Often dismissed as little more than a poetic adage, his words may need to be taken literally. If you think each strike can make the difference between life and death, you're likely to approach your training more seriously than a student who adopts a more lax attitude.

Not all fighting arts incorporate the idea of ikken hisatsu. Some may advocate slowly wearing down an opponent, inflicting a series of smaller injuries that eventually leave him incapacitated or force him to give up. There's something to be said for this approach, but it's not the one taken by karate. Ikken hisatsu reminds us of this, and it gives us much to think about in terms of our art.

# COMPASSION

*October 2004*

Some legends are so wonderful that you want them to be true. The legend of *bo* specialist Muso Gonnosuke's two meetings with Miyamoto Musashi is a good example. As a young man, Muso wandered around Japan challenging other martial artists to duels, both to make a name for himself and to perfect his art. Despite the risk of serious injury or death, he bested a number of skilled warriors with his staff.

While visiting the capital city of Edo (now Tokyo), Muso found Musashi, a renowned swordsman whose reputation was rapidly growing. Musashi was an unconventional fighter whose training in a formal *ryu* was rudimentary, but he used animal cunning, clever strategy and cool bravado to overcome his opponents. Indeed, in his duel with Muso, he didn't use a steel sword or even a wooden training weapon. Instead, he employed a tree limb to thoroughly and convincingly defeat his opponent—but he spared Muso's life.

Muso retreated to a mountaintop in Kyushu, where he trained furiously and meditated on his art and his loss. He was eventually rewarded with what he took to be a divine vision that compelled him to shorten his 6-foot-long staff. The modification enabled him to manipulate the weapon

---

*Hodoku* **is a central precept that elevates classical** *kata* **beyond simple physical exercise or mental training.**

---

like a sword and a spear while retaining its use as a staff.

Once again, he sought out Musashi and requested a rematch. Musashi obliged. This time, however, Muso was able to defeat his opponent. But just as Musashi had spared his life in their initial encounter, Muso let Musashi live, handing him—if the story is true—his only defeat.

More than four centuries later, Muso's descendants still practice the stick techniques he devised, which constitute part of the curriculum of *shindo muso ryu*, or *jojutsu* (art of the stick). Within the *kata* of the school are a range of lethal methods as well as examples of *hodoku*, or compassion, as shown by the founder of the ryu.

Whenever I hear people's petty arguments that Japanese terminology in the *dojo* should be replaced with English or other languages, I think of terms like "hodoku." I wonder what non-Japanese equivalent would be used, because the concept and its application would require pages of explanation.

Classical martial arts kata—which are almost always an exchange between two participants rather than the solo sequences with which most *karateka* are familiar—teach a variety of combative strategies. Some are long and complex, while others involve only a single attack and counter. Regardless of their length, once the forms are finished, both participants are left in potentially mortal situations. For example, your weapon is pointed directly at my throat, and mine is set to break your wrist. How do we resolve the standoff? We turn to an unlikely source: the terminology of Buddhism.

Buddhism has a word, *ko,* that's defined as being one moment longer than the longest stretch of time any human can comprehend. Perhaps our standoff wouldn't last that long, but in our positions and our attitudes, we must be in a state of ko. I'm willing to try to keep my advantage just as you're willing to try to keep yours.

In the dojo, the combative ko is broken when one participant voluntarily moves his weapon into a nonthreatening posture. Though he might still be in position to continue fighting, he shows a willingness to promote charity to his partner (which, of course, he would not do if the situation were real; in that case, ko is broken when one participant stops breathing). This attitude of compassion is hodoku.

In shindo muso ryu, one trainee is armed with a stick and the other wields a *bokken,* or wooden practice sword. At the conclusion of the kata, the swordsman slowly moves his weapon slightly off to his side, lowering it. This posture is called hodoku *kamae.* Slowly and carefully, without losing his concentration, the person with the stick slides his weapon back to a position at his side, responding in an equally humane way to the swordsman's charity. Both partners then retreat and assume positions for the next kata.

On one level, the process of hodoku is purely mechanical. The swordsman's lowering of his blade is a way to bring the kata to a technically safe conclusion. Even though the forms are precisely ritualized, they expose both practitioners to extreme danger. Weapons are swung with full force and stopped only at the last second, a fraction of an inch from a vulnerable target. Kata cannot be perfected without entering a mental state polished under the stresses of danger. Anything less and you'd just be dancing.

Given these concerns, a safe method for finishing a kata is important. But on a higher level, hodoku is a central precept that elevates classical kata beyond simple physical exercise or mental training. Equally as important as instilling combative skills, it imbues the form and its practice with humanity.

The sole purpose of kata in a traditional martial art is to teach and perfect the skills and attitudes necessary to destroy life efficiently. Nobody is trying to look beautiful or find inner peace. The kata are designed to teach killing or crippling, and anything else that may arise is purely secondary. Nevertheless, within the structure of the kata is built, in hodoku and other aspects of practice, the potential for great insight into human nature and the real meaning of what it is to fight.

It's all well and good to talk about the spiritual rewards of martial arts training and the martial ways and to teach their wonderful philosophical attributes. It's another thing entirely to include physical examples of these teachings in your daily practice. Shindo muso ryu does just that—as do, in one way or another, all the classical Japanese combative disciplines. And so the question you should ask yourself and your teacher is, Does my *budo* have hodoku within the kata or anywhere else in my training? Maybe a more crucial question is, Do I have the spirit of hodoku within myself?

# TOUGHING IT OUT

*November 2004*

Sometimes, martial arts enthusiasts are surprised to hear *sumo* referred to as a martial art. It certainly doesn't seem to fit in with karate, judo, *aikido* and the like. Sumo is still largely an unknown entity in this country. Our exposure to it has been limited to occasional snippets on the news played to amuse audiences as they mutter, "What a bizarre sport—fat guys in diapers pushing each other around."

In reality, sumo is centuries older than any other fighting art in Japan, and its traditions have influenced all the combat systems from that nation. Often, the practitioners of those styles are completely ignorant of where those traditions originated.

It's too bad more Westerners don't have a practical knowledge of sumo's techniques and a deeper understanding of its spirit. In Japan, where sumo was as popular as baseball until only recently, many young martial artists have a background in or at least some familiarity with the art. They've probably grappled informally or in school contests, and they know some of the techniques. This can give them a terrific advantage when they begin training in other forms of *budo*.

Young Japanese also benefit from having *sumotori* (sumo competitors) as role models. Despite the allegations of bout-fixing that have recently surfaced in the sumo world, the manner in which the wrestlers generally

---

**Like a samurai preparing for battle, the *sumotori* must put aside those feelings and control his natural tendency to want to crawl back into bed when he's ill.**

---

conduct themselves—especially during competitions—is one from which martial artists everywhere can learn a lot.

The professional sumo calendar includes six tournaments a year, each lasting 15 days, so athletes have 90 days of competition every year. Few professional sports demand that much of their participants.

For the sumotori, competition is very much like a battle, in that you can't just stay home if you don't feel well. If you don't compete at a tournament—even if you have a broken arm—you'll be demoted. You can apply to have a board of coaches review your claim, but even if they grant an appeal, you must enter the next tournament regardless of your condition

or risk losing your professional standing. That's why a sumotori has to be in extremely bad shape before he'll agree to go before the injury board.

There are many stories about sumotori who have competed under dire circumstances. For example, days before a tournament in September 1956, the 4-year-old son of then-grand champion Wakanohana was scalded to death in an accident. Most fans expected the wrestler to drop out of the competition, but he didn't. In the opening ceremony, he wore Buddhist prayer beads in remembrance of his son and went on to have a remarkable record of 12 consecutive wins. Just before the last day of the event, however, Wakanohana came down with a high fever and was forced to withdraw. Good as his record was for that tournament, the Sumo Association refused to go easy on him and decided that he hadn't compiled enough victories to be declared a *yokozuna* (grand champion). He was forced to compete in two more tournaments before he finally won that honor.

In 1989, one of the most outstanding champions of that decade, Chiyono-fuji, competed in and won a playoff on the last day of a tournament, despite the fact that his daughter had just died of sudden infant death syndrome.

Stories abound in the sporting world about athletes who have persevered under similarly trying circumstances. Still, there's something unique about the sumotori's challenge. He must go into the ring alone in front of millions of fans. If he fails, he can't shift the blame onto other members of the team. He must deal with not only the stress of competition but also the anxieties of combat. Being distracted by a personal problem—a fight with his wife, the death of a loved one or an illness—can mean more than just a loss. It's a good way to get seriously hurt. Like a samurai preparing for battle, the sumotori must put aside those feelings and control his natural tendency to want to crawl back into bed when he's ill. He must tough it out.

I'm not a warrior. I haven't participated in combat, and the fighting arts in which I've competed are nowhere near the level of professional sumo. Still, there are times when I must go out and take care of my responsibilities when I don't really want to. Occasionally I have to perform, just as you do, under circumstances that render me far below my best level. In those situations, I try to find inspiration in the sumotori. They've toughed it out in tough times. So can I, and so can you.

# CONTROLLING THE POINT
*December 2004*

The proficient swordsman understands that, to strike effectively, he must control the *kissaki*—the beveled tip—of his sword. To avoid being struck, he must also control the kissaki of his opponent's weapon. This strategy, which is taught from the moment he first picks up a blade, may initially seem to make little sense. After all, the sword is a long weapon, with an edge running nearly the full length of the blade. Why worry about that little pointy tip?

In fact, beginners generally focus all their energy on their fists as they hold the sword. If you tell them to point the tip at an opponent's throat, they'll keep it at that level for about five seconds. But then they shift their concentration to controlling their grip or stance, and the kissaki wanders.

This tendency is also of interest to the *karateka*. Although he may never pick up a sword, it's important for him to keep control of his kissaki to be successful in the ring or in self-defense.

Because neither the human arm nor leg is exactly analogous to a sword's tip, an unarmed fighter's kissaki is his centerline. For example, examine the fighting stance of a beginner. Invariably, you'll see an elbow sticking out, a foot turned in or out, or both fists either drooping or raised in front of his face. Conversely, the experienced fighter will have his fists, feet, elbows and knees aligned with the centerline of his body. His limbs are his weapons—the parts of his body that will make contact with his opponent. They are the kissaki he must control.

An adage in traditional Japanese swordsmanship holds that the kissaki's function is fourfold: It must touch the opponent, fend off attacks, press forward and provide what can best be translated as "springy resistance." The karateka's primary weapons—his hands and feet—perform exactly the same functions. They make contact with an opponent, touching or palpating in the course of the action to get feedback about his strengths and weaknesses, and to get a sense of how stiff or relaxed he is. They block attacks. They press in, seize or trap to set up a strike or prevent one. They fake and feint to distract.

Accomplishing these tasks is one of the principal components of learning karate, but it's impossible to master any of the fundamentals of combat without gaining competence in controlling your centerline and thus keeping your weapons ready for deployment.

Anyone who's ever practiced *kendo* knows that one of the most difficult

aspects of the art is forestalling or ignoring the fatigue that almost immediately sets in. If your combative experience has been empty-handed, you'll
be surprised at how quickly your arms become tired while holding even a
comparatively light weapon like a *shinai* (bamboo training sword). Your
arms begin to ache. Try though you might to hold it steady, the tip begins to
fall. Boxers know of this kind of weariness. Even if they're well-conditioned,
their arms often sink lower and lower as the match goes on.

Karateka tend to hold their fists a little lower than boxers do, so fatigue
might set in a little later. But it happens. That's one reason poorly trained
contestants at karate tournaments often turn away from their opponent
and fight while essentially facing the side. As they become more and more
fatigued, they gradually lose their ability to protect their centerline, and
they turn away owing to the unconscious fear of exposing it. The problem is
that they must maintain that centerline to deliver their attacks. That's why
so many contests turn into slapping matches, with weak kicks and backfists that take a wide, circular path to the target. Only the expert *kendoka*,
boxer or karateka can keep his weapons on the centerline and in position
to constantly cover and threaten his opponent throughout the fight.

The ability to control the kissaki—or, in the case of the karateka, to
control the centerline by keeping his fists and feet properly aligned on
it—is a big advantage when it comes to offense. When his hands are where
they should be, there's a minimum of wasted motion that can telegraph
his intentions and drain his energy. Watch how a good karateka holds his
posture during a fight. His fists are nearly always pointing directly at his
opponent, and his feet are slightly off the centerline so his hips are aimed
at the target. His knees and elbows are relaxed, but they're still close to
the centerline so he can unleash kicks and punches from either side of his
body directly at the target.

There's no easy or quick way to learn to control your kissaki. It requires
physical conditioning and good instruction in the fundamentals of stance
and movement. Therefore, it's a good idea to videotape yourself during a
match so you can see where you're able to maintain a good line and where
you falter.

Many swordsmen from the old days of Japan could discern all they
needed to know about an opponent by touching the kissaki of his sword.
They could tell whether he was too stiff or too relaxed, or whether he was
inadvertently signaling an attack. Much of what you need to know to size
up an opponent in the *dojo* can also be discovered by paying attention to
his kissaki.

# FIRST IMPRESSIONS

*January 2005*

K arate and judo practitioners rarely wear them, but for exponents of martial arts like *aikido, kendo* and *kyudo,* the experience of getting into a *hakama* for the first time is often memorable. It's something like being enveloped in a cloth sea of pleats.

Hakama are skirt-like pants that were part of daily wear for men during Japan's feudal age. Now they're worn primarily on formal occasions like weddings and during the practice of traditional arts like the tea ceremony or the *budo.* Because of their billowing, often-confusing array of pleats and creases, more than one beginner has put his hakama on backward so the *koshi-ita,* or stiff hip board, is around his abdomen. (Watch for this in old Chinese kung fu movies in which the Japanese are inevitably the bad guys and are often portrayed in an unintentionally comical way.)

Today, hakama used for martial arts practice are often made of polyester blends that hold their creases well. But the training hakama worn in the *dojo* when I was a youngster were made entirely of natural cotton. They held their creases as poorly as Madonna holds a tune. They had to be folded exactly right after a workout to keep the creases and pleats straight and neat

---

**I eventually learned that *orime tadashii* has a connotation beyond its literal meaning: By paying attention to small things like the creases in your *hakama,* you develop a sense of propriety.**

---

and to prevent wrinkles. Because I wore one almost every day, I got good at the art of folding the hakama. One of the first expressions I learned in Japanese was *orime tadashii,* which roughly means "correctly creased."

It isn't just in folding a hakama to put it away that its creases must be kept in order. While wearing one, there are ways of sitting and standing that will keep it neat. It's not a coincidence that these same postures and motions all have a martial application in that they tend to be the best ways of maintaining a relaxed state of vigilance. And so I eventually learned that orime tadashii has a connotation beyond its literal meaning: By paying attention to small things like the creases in your hakama, you develop a sense of propriety.

It may not be one of the most pressing problems in the martial arts and ways right now, but it seems to me that most practitioners are neither cultivating within themselves nor encouraging among their fellow practitioners a sense of orime tadashii. There is too little emphasis on neatness or attention to detail—not only in the dojo but also in life outside it.

Not long ago, I was walking through an airport when I saw a martial arts celebrity, who was apparently catching a connecting flight. I'd never met him, but I recognized his face from the many photos I've seen. It took me a moment, however, because I was so surprised by his appearance: dirty sneakers, no shirt and a pair of farmer's overalls that were ragged and stained. He looked like a bum. Now, my wardrobe hardly qualifies me to be among the gods of fashion, but that's not what we're talking about. What we're talking about is having enough self-respect to keep yourself clean and presentable in public. What we're talking about is a sense of orime tadashii.

Orime tadashii is not the same as being foppish. It's not, as I have seen some martial artists do, about insisting on training in a silk kimono and a hakama. I'm afraid those folks have confused the martial arts with *kabuki* performances. I was recently told about a fellow who came to a seminar devoted to some form of *jujutsu*. He arrived wearing the costume I just described, along with a folded fan stuck in his belt. That's dangerous to be wearing while taking falls, he was warned, but he insisted that this was "proper" and set about practicing. Then he took a fall that caused his knee to come flying up, striking the butt of the fan and stabbing it into his stomach. He turned white and, gasping for breath, staggered off to the sidelines to observe the rest of the session.

There's a common male mentality in this country which holds that too much attention to one's personal appearance is not masculine. I share it. Orime tadashii, however, isn't the same as prissiness or vanity or sartorial affectation. It's a simple, unassuming dignity that's reflected in the way you dress and conduct yourself. It's a preference for neatness. I knew a karate student who, for some reason, could never figure out that his uniform needed washing just as would any other garment that gets dirty. He'd train hard, and his uniform would be soaked with sweat. It would go directly into a bag, which was dumped into the trunk of his car. It would sit there until he retrieved it a couple of days later when he returned to work out. He wasn't a slob in general; it was just that he couldn't see anything wrong with wearing a stinking, wrinkled uniform. He had no concept of orime tadashii.

To reiterate, I won't be posing for the cover of *GQ* anytime soon. But whether I like it or not, I'm a representative of the martial arts in the eyes of the public. And so are you. If we're known among friends and family members as martial arts exponents, they'll arrive at certain conclusions about our arts based on us. That can include our general appearance.

There are those who will insist it's nit-picking to be concerned with superficial details. "Maybe I look like a slob on the outside, but inside, I'm neat and tidy, and that's all that counts," they insist. Orime tadashii, they might argue, can be a deserved pejorative to describe those who fuss too much over trivialities. Perhaps that's the case here.

However, maybe paying attention to the creases is a small step in the right direction for our arts. If you'd seen that guy at the airport, I think you'd agree that a little more attention to orime tadashii wouldn't hurt anyone.

# THE NEXT FUNAKOSHI?

*February 2005*

I recently received a letter from a "Master Smith," who advised me that crafting an article about him would be a tremendous asset to *Black Belt* and a boost to my career as a writer. Painstakingly handwritten, his list of reasons for doing the story filled two pages. One of the accomplishments he mentioned was that he'd founded his own style. He noted several awards he'd received, along with a lengthy tabulation of his tournament victories. He wasn't bashful. He said that, if I were "interested in a fabulous story of a man who has come far in a total mastery of martial arts," I could do no better than to call immediately to arrange to interview him for a story.

My initial reaction was that he'd probably never read one of my columns. I detest interviewing people I admire, let alone total strangers. My writing is devoted almost exclusively to the traditional martial arts, which leaves out people who call themselves "master." Such individuals populate a different planet than the one I'm on in terms of our views on the combative arts. I grew up with a philosophy of *budo* that's foreign to Smith. Were we to have a conversation, we wouldn't even speak the same language.

Still shaking my head over Smith's letter, I considered a biography I was reading about Gichin Funakoshi. Many traditionalists regard the founder of modern Japanese karate to be the art's patron saint; they

---

**While Funakoshi and his colleagues in early 20th-century Japan sought to change karate deliberately, Smith's innovations are largely the byproduct of a whim.**

---

would surely put him at the opposite end of the spectrum from Smith. But I wondered whether there really was that much difference between these two martial artists.

In a sense, there isn't. Funakoshi took an Okinawan folk art and transformed it exhaustively. Using a foreign (from the Okinawan perspective) culture, he translated karate into something very different from what it had been. Some Okinawan practitioners of *tode* would scarcely have recognized their art after only a couple of decades of the innovations wrought by Funakoshi and others on the Japanese mainland. He adapted karate, made it palatable—both culturally and socially—for the Japanese appetite. He was so successful that many of its senior exponents in Japan today are positively indignant if you suggest that karate isn't really Japanese.

A generation later, Smith is similarly transforming karate from a purely Asian discipline into one that's more accessible to Western practitioners. Just as when it was transplanted from Okinawan to Japan, inevitably something will be lost. Westernized karate has very little of the dignity found in the traditional budo. For example, one of the photos Smith sent with his letter shows him posing shirtless, with muscles bulging like a professional wrestler. The letter also revealed a remarkable ego—self-promoting and bereft of the reticence and dignity associated with the traditional arts.

However, it would be a mistake to dismiss Smith and his kind out of hand. For one thing, he looks like one tough character, and I have little doubt he can fight. He focuses on the effectiveness of karate as a fighting skill; while you may believe he's being too narrow in this regard, it's foolish to deny he's getting something he considers valuable from his practice. It's also unrealistic to think he represents an aberration in the martial arts when those trying to preserve karate's traditional roots are the ones in the minority.

Smith is changing karate to meet his needs and those of a different culture, just as Funakoshi did years ago. Japanese karate is even more popular, better known and more influential than its Okinawan predecessor. In fact, a good argument could be made that popularizing karate in Japan and elsewhere has been the impetus for many *karateka* to go back to the art's Okinawan roots and revitalize them.

So, is Smith any different from Funakoshi? The Okinawan master translated karate into a Japanese context, just as the Westerner is translating it into a Western construct. However, Funakoshi was born and raised in the original culture of karate. The changes he implemented were from the perspective of someone with a grasp of what the martial art was before he set out to make it into something new. Conversely, Smith knows virtually nothing of how karate was traditionally taught. He doesn't speak the language or understand many of its cultural connotations. (You might disagree with this opinion and note that those are superfluous to what he wants to do, but isn't it better to be equipped with stuff you might need and later find out you don't, than the other way around?)

Funakoshi and other Okinawan teachers transformed karate when they brought it to Japan, but they did so with a reasonably strong and clear sense of where they came from. They weren't entirely sure of where they were going, which is evident in the mistakes and blunders, however well-intentioned, they made along the way. But they could retrace their steps, if necessary, and return to where they started. Having set out on a similar journey, Smith and his kind don't have this advantage. They've begun a reformation with only the vaguest idea of what karate is or was in the first place.

What's worse is that, while Funakoshi and his colleagues in early 20th-century Japan sought to change karate deliberately, Smith's innovations are largely the byproduct of a whim. He likes a kick he saw in *taekwondo*, so he adds it. Brazilian grappling skills appeal to him, so he dumps them into the pot, as well. Lacking a strong underlying foundation, his art is mostly a hodgepodge of what he fancies.

But who knows? Perhaps someday karate students will have Master Smith's picture displayed in a place of honor at the front of the *dojo* and genuflect to his memory. It could happen. It's certainly more likely than my interviewing him for this column.

# HEROES
*March 2005*

What sort of heroes do young martial artists have today? I suppose it would be action stars who employ the Asian fighting arts in movies. When I was a boy, our heroes in the martial arts tended to be those who actually were accomplished martial artists. One of mine was a judo champion named Kyuzo Mifune.

Mifune died in 1965, four years before I began judo. But in the late '60s, he still cast a long shadow over the art. Those of us who practiced judo saw films of him in action. In those old 16 mm reels, he conducted free practice with guys half his age, throwing them at will and never once succumbing to their best efforts to upend him.

We trained with many of Mifune's direct students. All of us, especially small guys like me, studied his methods constantly. His *Canon of Judo* was beautifully bound with the thick cloth of a judo *gi*, and I remember copies of it that were worn and frayed from use. I think a lot of his appeal was that he was so small. In his prime, he was just 5 feet 3 inches tall and weighed 110 pounds. In spite of that, there was no question he was the

---

**In his prime, [Mifune] was just 5 feet 3 inches tall and weighed 110 pounds. In spite of that, there was no question he was the finest tactician judo ever produced.**

---

finest tactician judo ever produced. In a career that spanned five decades, he was never beaten.

We heard endless stories about Mifune, who was reportedly a training fanatic. We were told he sometimes napped in the rafters of his home, stretched out on a wooden crossbeam. The practice allowed him to perfect his balance; and if he happened to roll over and go down, it gave him a chance to polish his skills for landing on his feet when thrown.

Less legendary was Mifune's role in introducing *kakari-geiko* to judo. Defined as "attack training," it involves lining up several partners to engage in *randori*, or free practice. One guy goes three minutes with a partner, then bows and takes on the next man for another three, on and on down the line. Kakari-geiko is a splendid way to improve aerobic fitness and build fighting spirit. Faced with multiple opponents, all of them more rested than you, you must act quickly. There cannot be a lot of dancing around while you look for an opening. Each person must be met and thrown as quickly as possible.

Mifune's intensive training paid off. Some of his contests became judo legends. He was such a furious competitor that even one of his rare ties, in a bout in 1907, was still being retold six decades later.

Mifune was nursing an injured leg at the time, sitting on the side of the mat at the Kodokan, watching a practice session. "Hey, Mifune! You too tired to train?" It was Hidekazu Nagaoka, a fifth *dan* and one of the tigers of the Kodokan.

Despite his injury, Mifune, a fourth dan, rose to his feet in an instant. He and Nagaoka came to grips, and Nagaoka showed no mercy. Just as one would take advantage of the weakness of an enemy on the battlefield, he exploited Mifune's injury, immediately going after the leg with a vicious reap. Mifune said later he nearly fainted from the pain. Still, he managed to stay on his feet and muster a counter to Nagaoka's attack.

Using a similar strategy, Mifune came in with a sweep of his own. He used his injured leg for the throw, hoping to catch Nagaoka unaware. The technique nearly worked. Nagaoka and Mifune both fell to the mat, engaging in an all-out grappling match. It required one of their seniors to step in and stop the escalating workout.

Technically, the bout between Nagaoka and Mifune was a draw. When *judoka* get together, however, and the subject comes up, most are inclined to give Mifune the credit for having bested Nagaoka because he fought a higher-ranked exponent to a draw.

A number of the techniques still seen in judo practice sessions and tournaments were either created by Mifune or perfected by him. Perhaps his most famous throw was *uki-otoshi*, the "floating drop." While grasping an opponent's collar and sleeve in the *kumi-kata* hold, the thrower retreats and, as he's followed, drops to one knee, twisting his hips and using the opponent's forward momentum to accomplish a throw that's spectacular. With what looks like nothing more than the proverbial "twist of the wrists," the opponent is projected through the air like a sack of flour.

This technique is rarely seen in tournaments anymore; most competitive judoka are unable to perfect the timing and subtle off-balancing needed to perform it. Mifune may have been the only judo practitioner ever to make it work in competition. When he did, it was amazing.

It happened in 1930. Mifune was nearly 50 and a seventh dan. His opponent was Kaichiro Samura, also ranked at seventh degree. The event was the first All-Japan Judo Championships in Tokyo, and their bout lasted more than 20 minutes. In the end, it was Mifune who prevailed, throwing Samura decisively with an uki-otoshi.

Another legendary match took place with an American during the U.S. occupation of Japan. Most Japanese *budo* were outlawed by military authorities right after the war. In part because of the interest shown by American soldiers, however, the ban was gradually lifted. At a formal demonstration of judo, Mifune was approached by an officer who politely but firmly insisted that what he was doing just couldn't be real. Mifune, despite being an old man, still had the same fighting spirit he'd demonstrated in the contest with Nagaoka. He invited the man to step onto the mat. The officer accepted, but just before they began, he laughingly told Mifune he was in poor shape and asked Mifune not to throw him. Mifune agreed.

The match commenced, and the officer tried wrestling throws and some of the rudimentary skills of hand-to-hand combat he'd learned. Mifune stayed with him like a shadow. At times, it looked as though the officer was going to hoist Mifune overhead and heave him to the mat, but Mifune always managed to twist and land on his feet. Or cling to the back of the officer. Or dodge away at the last second. Eventually, the officer, red-faced and panting, called a halt to the activity. Others in attendance were quick to point out, laughing, that Mifune had certainly honored the request and not thrown the man.

Kyuzo Mifune lived during something of a renaissance for the Japanese martial arts. Tremendous advances were made in the development of *aikido*, modern karate, *kendo* and judo. He was gone, as I said, by the time I began my own training, but his memory lived on brightly in the martial artists of my generation—little guys who dreamed of becoming the sort of master he was.

# BLACK BELT
## P R E S E N T S

# JAPANESE ARTS
## Books and DVDs

### JO:
### Art of the Japanese Short Staff
*by Dave Lowry*
This book teaches the art of the *jo*, the simple short staff that defeated the great swordsman Musashi. Topics include history, fundamentals, combinations, the traditional 31-count form and applications against a swordsman. Dave Lowry is a noted scholar and practitioner of Japanese weaponry. Fully illustrated. 192 pgs. (ISBN 0-89750-116-0) **Book Code 455—Retail $14.95**

### BOKKEN:
### Art of the Japanese Sword
*by Dave Lowry*
Author Dave Lowry of the ancient sword school *Yagyu Shinkage-Ryu* teaches the basics of Japanese swordsmanship using the *bokken*, the wooden training sword. Lowry covers stances, body movement, striking, combination techniques and techniques with a partner. Fully illustrated. 192 pgs. (ISBN 0-89750-104-7) **Book Code 443—Retail $14.95**

### SMALL-CIRCLE JUJITSU
*by Wally Jay*
The complete system of small-circle *jujitsu*. Fully illustrated, this book covers falling, key movements, resuscitation, all forms of joint locks, throwing techniques, chokes and self-defense applications. Professor Jay is a member of *Black Belt's* Hall of Fame. 256 pgs. (ISBN 0-89750-122-5)
**Book Code 462—Retail $17.95**

### SMALL-CIRCLE JUJITSU
*by Wally Jay*
Professor Wally Jay is a *Black Belt* Hall of Fame member (1969), 10th-*dan* in *jujitsu* under Juan Gomez (a top disciple of Henry S. Okazaki) and a sixth dan in judo under Ken Kawachi. Jay is one of the few martial artists this century to have come up with a theory of fighting, developed it and put it into practice. His influence is felt throughout the martial arts industry.
**Volume 1** discusses the 10 basic principles of small-circle *jujitsu*, including an explanation and demonstration of finger, wrist and joint locking. (Approx. 40 min.) **DVD Code 4089—Retail $34.95**
**Volume 2** discusses in-depth advanced arm, wrist, finger and leg locks. (Approx. 40 min.) **DVD Code 4099—Retail $34.95**
**Volume 3** discusses grappling, including falling, effective throws, advanced chokes and resuscitation. (Approx. 40 min.) **DVD Code 5119—Retail $34.95**
**Volume 4** discusses the principles of learning the tendon tricep and its importance in the application of armbars and arm locks. (Approx. 50 min.) **DVD Code 7459—Retail $34.95**
**Volume 5** discusses the principles of learning highly effective finger-locking techniques for self-defense application. (Approx. 50 min.) **DVD Code 7469—Retail $34.95**
*Buy all 5 DVDs for $139.80—Code X141*

### SHITO-RYU KARATE
*by Fumio Demura*
Striking points, target areas, stances, hand, elbow and foot techniques, and methods of blocking are covered in this fully illustrated book on *shito-ryu*, one of the four major styles of Japanese karate. 96 pgs. (ISBN 0-89750-005-9) **Book Code 110—Retail $12.95**

### KARATE
*by Fumio Demura*
*Black Belt* Hall of Fame member and former JKFA director Fumio Demura is an expert on traditional weapons and considered one of the best karate instructors in the world.
**Volume 1** includes striking points, target areas, standing positions and hand, elbow, kicking and blocking techniques, basic sparring and self-defense. (Approx. 90 min.) **DVD Code 1049—Retail $29.95**
**Volume 2** includes body dynamics, flexibility training, self-defense training, blocks, stances, striking, leg techniques, sparring and five *kata*. (Approx. 60 min.) **DVD Code 6079—Retail $29.95**
**Volume 3** includes senior and black-belt-level *kata* and self-defense techniques; judo throws; punches, elbows, chops, kicks and other techniques; and kata (*naifanchin shodan, matsumura rohai, sanchin, jitte, bassai dai* and *jiin*). (Approx. 60 min.) **DVD Code 6089—Retail $29.95**
**Volume 4** includes special breathing exercise; sparring drills; *unsoku, bunkai* and *oyo*; and black-belt-level *kata* (*naifanchin nidan, jion, niseishi [nijushi ho], wanshu [empi], kusankui dai [kosukun dai]* and *wankari*). (Approx. 60 min.) **DVD Code 6099—Retail $29.95**
**Volume 5** includes how to develop bigger, better and more powerful kicking techniques; black-belt-level drills; self-defense techniques; and *kata* (*naifanchin san dan, seienshin, aoyagi* [men's version], aoyagi [women's version], *seipai* and *juroku*). (Approx. 60 min.) **DVD Code 7119—Retail $29.95**
*Buy all 5 DVDs for $119.80—Code X153*

### KEIJUTSUKAI AIKIDO:
### Japanese Art of Self-Defense
*by Thomas Makiyama*
Thomas Makiyama, an eighth-degree black belt and the only American officially certified *shihan* by any Japanese *aikido* organization, teaches preparation, basic directional throws, classification forms, and basic and advanced self-defense. Fully illustrated. 176 pgs. (ISBN 0-89750-092-X)
**Book Code 428—Retail $15.95**

### KEIJUTSUKAI AIKIDO:
### Japanese Art of Self-Defense
*by Thomas H. Makiyama*
Learn 40 intermediate and advanced techniques, extensions, modifications and step-by-step elaboration of fundamentals. Great for beginners and experts! (Approx. 60 min.) **DVD Code 1069—Retail $29.95**

## To order, call 1-800-581-5222 or visit www.blackbeltmag.com